Charles Linden's
Stress Free in
30 Days

Other Titles by Charles Linden

The Linden Method for Anxiety, Panic Attacks & Phobias
ISBN 0954980301

The Linden Method (Junior Version)
ISBN 095498031X

Conquer Anxiety & Panic Attacks DVD
ISBN 0954980352

Conquering Generalized Anxiety Disorder (GAD) DVD
ISBN 0954980360

Conquering Panic Disorder & Panic Attacks DVD
ISBN 0954980387

Conquering Obsessive Compulsive Disorder (OCD) DVD
ISBN 0954980379

Conquering Agoraphobia & Social Phobia DVD
ISBN 0954980395

Stress Free in 30 Days

Charles Linden

LifeWise Publishing Ltd. The Ashlane Centre. Worcester Road. Kidderminster. DY10 1JR

ISBN 978-0-9556568-0-4

Book production by Action Publishing Technology Ltd.
Printed in Great Britain

Contents

Dedicated to my mum, dad and grandma
Kathleen Florence Lampitt
1911–2005.

Foreword

We all experience work and life pressure at some point during our lives and whilst some people thrive on these pressures, others can eventually fall to pieces physically and emotionally.

Staying together in stressful times isn't about physical or mental strength; it is partly to do with emotional intelligence but mostly to do with perception.

Whilst one person might perceive their situation as dire, another might perceive that situation as exciting or challenging; others might find it as dull as ditch water.

We are all different, all the product of our individual environments, our experiences and our genetics. Whilst genetics play a definite role in determining our familiar predispositions to certain traits or conditions, our environments as we pass through life have the most dramatic influence on how we react emotionally and physically under any given situation.

If those who experience stress could simply change their subconscious reaction to that stress by altering their perception of it, the physical and mental affect of stress would dissipate completely.

Stress can have far reaching and invasive consequences. Sufferers often experience anxiety disorders, phobias, panic attacks or depressive thoughts; but with a slight alteration in their perception, stress and all of the symptoms it brings with it, can be eliminated or avoided completely.

Charles Linden and The Linden Method

Charles Linden was born in the UK in 1968 and now lives in Worcestershire with his wife Beth and their children Charles and Florence.

Throughout his life, from early childhood, Charles suffered from stress and anxiety conditions which finally manifested themselves in early adulthood as anxiety and panic disorder with agoraphobia.

Charles struggled with his condition for many years, visiting practitioners to try to overcome his troubles. For many months, Charles would be housebound, drug dependent and unable to work or function 'normally'. Using medication and conventional psychotherapies seemed ineffectual as he became dependent on his medications, especially the tranquilisers which required constant dose increases to produce any affect at all.

Having visited every possible practitioner in order to find a solution, or at least a treatment which would allow him to function somewhat normally, Charles decided that he could no longer rely on conventional practitioners to provide an answer they seemed incapable of supplying.

Feeling abandoned by the medical world, Charles set about a personal programme of research and discovery which would lead to the solution which cured him within weeks and has since helped tens of thousands of sufferers from all around the world to overcome their anxiety, stress and depression permanently.

The solution Charles discovered, called *The Linden Method*, is the exact same pathway which all recovered sufferers have followed to become well again. Charles' Method and the support provided by *The Linden Method* specialists provide the structure, guidance and support required to implement the solution correctly in order for sufferers to make a fast and permanent recovery.

Charles runs The Linden Centres, implementing *The Linden Method* with the assistance of his team of counsellors and psychologists who provide constant support to clients all around the world.

In addition to *The Linden Method* and this book, Charles has published a number of DVD titles and heads up a corporate stress and anxiety elimination programme called Stress Away.

For more information about *The Linden Method*, visit www.stopworry.com

For more information about Charles' other products, visit www.karmamind.com

Introduction

Congratulations on taking your first step towards eliminating stress and worry from your life … permanently!

I guarantee that by following our guidelines and suggestions, you WILL SEE RESULTS in less than 30 days. And if you continue using the guidelines and tips that you receive throughout this 'Boot Camp', you will be able to manage your stress and worry much more effectively, because you will understand the key secrets of creating lasting balance in the bodily systems which control how you feel. This programme is a 30-day plan but, hopefully, most of what you learn you will take with you for the rest of your life.

During these 30 days I will recommend certain products. These recommendations are based on the testimonials of many people who have benefited massively from them. Many of these products I will also have used myself. Whether you choose to follow my recommendations is entirely your decision.

In order to eliminate stress, anxiety and worry from your life, you need to be READY to make some changes in your life practices; the way you think and the way that you behave.

This is a 'one size fits all' programme designed to bring balance to your physical and mental self and it is time and user tested, distilled from piles of the most relevant information and delivered to you in an easy to use and potent format.

I know that everyone wants a 'magic pill', a 'quick fix' remedy that can be swallowed in seconds with immediate results, this simply doesn't exist. Stress, anxiety and worry are behaviourally based; they result from your inability to cope successfully with life pressures. We are going to change all that.

We can help to eliminate the physical symptoms by rebalancing your bodily systems; we will show you how to create balance in your daily routines and how to STOP worry in its path.

We realise that every person is different physically and emotionally as well as having very different routines, goals and ambitions; but this is irrelevant. By implementing structure in every element of your life, you can quickly eliminate those things which cause you most emotional and physical harm … it's all about balance and perception. Balance in the body and mind and your perception of your situation. If you feel overwhelmed by work for example, chances are that you aren't managing your time efficiently. The only way to combat this is to implement behavioural 'tactics' to create balance and to change your perception of the situation at hand ... you either see it as a stressor or a challenge ... it's your choice, BUT, one produces positive change, one perpetuates negativity.

This programme is implemented by following the instructions in each chapter in turn. I can't force you to do the things I suggest, you may even feel that they are futile, however, trust me, having helped tens of thousands of people worldwide, our research is pretty conclusive. The structure we will suggest to you can and will bring about many positive changes, permanent ones which will create a solid foundation on which to build the challenges, dreams and achievements of your life to come.

Some days the instructions might be quite simple to implement, others may be more difficult; please try to comply as closely as possible. Some days the instructions may not be relevant to you, if that is the case, don't do them ... it's that simple.

You are now well prepared to commence the journey into the rest of your life – stress, anxiety and worry free. I suggest you start to read and implement my advice immediately.

I recommend some supportive and informative products along the way and give web addresses of where you can acquire them, most of which are through my website www.karmamind.com; not because I am a crazed internet salesman, but because I have assembled a database of the most useful products and services we have tried and tested over the years. Instead of sending you off aimlessly shopping for good deals, I thought it best to make them available to you with minimal effort. If you still feel like shopping around, feel free.

What is stress?

First of all, let's discover the kind of things which cause stress. Stress can be caused by anything which creates an imbalance in your practical and emotional life. This could be bereavement, work pressure, financial worries, health concerns, bullying, or any number of other issues, no matter how insignificant to others, which impact on your 'life practices' and/or emotions.

Stress is the negative manifestation of 'life pressure'. Life pressure can be caused by any one of the examples we have just mentioned but these are not stress, they are the normal and expected issues we confront in life; however, we all react differently and our tolerance to such issues differs massively from one person to another. What is one person's passion could be another person's poison. Base jumping doesn't fill me with exhilaration, but for many people it's a walk in the park! Some people seem to thrive on challenges which increase their anxiety levels. Many people develop anxiety disorders, panic attacks or other behavioural conditions when experiencing similar levels of physical and emotional stress.

Please don't think that this is a sign of weakness. Many stress and anxiety sufferers find themselves suffering precisely **because** they are so strong, the weaker people tend to drop out of the race early on, due to a kind of 'self preservation' response which prevents them from pushing themselves too far. Stress and anxiety sufferers tend to be strong and able, intelligent and driven.

Stress can be good for us in controlled doses but when the stress is relentless, it no longer drives ambition, but produces unpleasant and sometimes very frightening physical and psychological symptoms.

It isn't uncommon for people to become 'stress chasers'. Like storm chasers, these people look for trouble and thrive on the challenges of overcoming it. Many recovered stress and anxiety sufferers develop an attitude of *"I've been to hell and back and now I have tamed the monster, I am going to exploit it!"*

What are the physical manifestations of stress?

The most obvious physical manifestations during periods of stress are chemical initially. Hormonal changes in the hypothalamus, which cause reactions in the pituitary glands in the brain, cause the adrenal glands to release adrenalin (epinephrine) into the blood stream.

Adrenalin is the hormone which regulates the anxiety response; often called the 'fight or flight' response. This response is activated in times of 'real' danger which would cause us to either fight or run from that danger.

When this mechanism developed in the human body, it was designed to prepare the body to go into combat with fierce animals for example, or, if combat was futile, to run away at least.

It has been some time since Sabre Tooth Tigers roamed the land, but the anxiety response has become more useful to cope with near crashes, bar room brawls, work strain and other such wonders of modern life.

The problem is that the human body hasn't had time to adjust or evolve with the differences between prehistoric and modern life, so the anxiety response is still very unrefined and sometimes very inappropriate. It is especially inappropriate when it reacts under circumstances such as life or work stress, where the extreme 'fight or flight' response is 'overkill'.

Environmental stimuli from the sensory organs collect information about the potential threat and feed those signals back to the brain, more specifically the hippocampus and the amygdala. This should under 'normal', appropriate circumstances, provide the brain with enough information to enable it to react appropriately to the situation at hand … but it doesn't always work out that way.

When stressful life circumstances repeatedly produce this kind of reaction and regularly raise the anxiety and stress levels above the 'normal' preset levels, changes happen in the amygdala which cause it to become 'stuck' at a much higher level of reaction. The 'benchmark' level of stress or anxiety which triggers this response is lowered, meaning that the sufferer becomes more reactive under much less threatening circumstances.

The brain is like a computer ... but, with one difference.

The brain stores and release information like a computer, but unlike computers which store information in file systems, 'brain learning' happens through building 'new' file systems; these are called neural pathways. Neural pathways build constantly in the brain; they are the building blocks of memory, physical and mental response and learning. As the anxious 'habit' forms, the brain quickly builds new neural pathways for this new behaviour and labels them as 'NORMAL'.

When we feel anxious or stressed as a result of these changes, we know that they are wrong, but the brain thinks they are completely normal.

Stress and anxiety breeds stress and anxiety.

As we experience escalating stress and anxiety, we become weakened emotionally and physically and very soon, a cycle of fear and stress can become the 'norm'.

Physical makeup and genetics dictate, to a certain extent, how we react during these times and it is said that some people have a genetic predisposition to such problems; however, I believe that environment and emotional intelligence are primarily responsible for stress and anxiety conditions and this theory is strongly reinforced by our experience over many years helping many tens of thousands of people with such issues.

Of course, it is important to understand that some people may not have access to the level of support which others may have. Some sufferers are alone with their condition, either due to a lack of family support or a lack of emotional attachment to those who might otherwise help them through such difficult times.

Our ability to interact with others can have a knock on affect through family, work and social experiences and can heavily influence a sufferer's reaction to stressors and anxiety provoking situations. These factors can also have quite a profound affect on our own self image and self confidence which, in turn, can affect our social behaviours, alcohol consumption, diet, drug abuse and many other factors.

Psychological development

Throughout life, as we take the twists, turns, highs and lows it presents us with, we adapt and learn from each and every experience. Some people cope and adapt better than others and this can be due to previous life experience, adopting the behaviours of others or guidance from another party.

Regardless of whether or not you have a genetic predisposition to stress related conditions, the reason you are suffering right now is purely dependent on your perception of the situations which have given rise to the initial stress. It is vital you understand this. How you see your situation, regardless of whether you are seeing it accurately or inaccurately, is irrelevant; what is important is that you can change that perception through training your mind to react more appropriately to stressors. Stress can be eliminated and so can all the physical conditions which it causes, such as panic attacks, OCD, phobias and all of the physical sensations, disturbed thoughts or emotions you may be experiencing.

The good news is that through a structured stress elimination programme, some 'common sense' behaviour modifications, knowledge and reassurance you can and will be stress free once again.

Recap

- Stress is the physical manifestation of work pressure
- Stress can create changes in the body which can feel frightening and unpleasant
- Stress is a learned response to negative behaviours, thoughts and perceived danger
- Some people thrive on stress – some don't
- You will be stress free once again – stress is a transient state

So how do you create balance?

The level or type of stress experienced can not only affect one person more radically than the next, but can also cause a very different physical and mental manifestation. This is usually mainly dependent on what else is going on in their life or with their health, job or relationship at that time. A combination of badly timed events can come together and create a reaction which, at other times, would never have happened.

The ratio of 'stressful event' : 'ability to cope' fluctuates throughout our lives and sometimes it takes something as simple as a common cold to knock us sideways and cause a cascade of bad fortune, stress and emotion.

Because our reaction to an event is vital to the impact that event has on our lives, you must understand that by modifying the way you respond, you can change the impact! It stands to reason.

When we are confronted by a potential stressor, we make a decision on how to react based on what we perceive through our sensory organs – subconsciously. We may experience an uncontrollable anxiety response and experience the familiar symptoms of fear, BUT, our conscious reaction to that stressor can be controlled. Some people allow their subconscious mind to lead them to a decision, others are more measured, more controlled and make a more intelligent decision before responding; emotional intelligence is a disadvantage at this point and it is those with high levels of emotional intelligence who generally suffer most. Unfortunately for stress sufferers, those who respond more appropriately at these times are people who generally have a lower emotional response to everything in life. Patience and self control are key here, even when it goes against your normal behaviour to be that way.

Making the decision about how to react, is what I call a 'binary decision'. Binary is the digital language used by computers … binary is like a mathematical switch – computers calculate things by asking questions – is the answer a 1 or a 0? If it's a 1, it switches one way, if it's a 0, it switches the other. Having a cold is putting you into a binary state – you either have a cold or you don't, it's either a 1 or a 0! So, how you respond consciously to anything is a binary decision – you can either take route 1 or route 0.

You see, there is a formula that is followed by the mind when confronted by a stressful event.

Event → Our response to that event (emotional or physical) → It's impact on us

So depending on how you perceive the impact of an event, depends on how you react and manage the outcome of that event and how you then cope with any consequences of that event.

To a person like me with children, a mortgage and car payments, loss of my income would seem catastrophic. To a single person living at home and driving dad's car when they need it, the consequences of a job loss would be emotional, but nonetheless, a whole lot less significant.

But, why should it be? If I were to lose my income tomorrow, I could perceive it as a massive blow, or I could perceive it as an opportunity to take on new challenges or change career. The whole experience may, at first, appear impossible or catastrophic, but with careful management, structure and thought, it could be a blessing in disguise … it's all down to perception. Fear is built from 'catastrophic' thought processes or 'what if?' thoughts. These same thoughts fuel anxiety disorders.

The fear of consequences can be overwhelming and can cause people to develop some pretty damaging 'self preservation' techniques such as agoraphobia or social phobia, which, when they work, provide a damaging cocoon for the sufferer; when they try to leave the cocoon, they experience high levels of anxiety and maybe even panic attacks. This is caused by 'false fear' … fear of something that hasn't, or may never, happen.

Recap

- Our stress levels are a direct response to our ability to deal with whatever demands are placed on us.

- The conscious part of that process is based on us making binary decisions – we either decide to cope, or we don't.

- Stress can lead to the development of other physical and mental conditions if not dealt with correctly.

There are a number of life circumstances which are most cited as the source of their stress. The list includes:

- **Divorce**
- **Moving home**
- **Bereavement**
- **Pregnancy or hormone issues**
- **Loss of a job**
- **Changed lifestyle/move to another area or country**
- **Work stress**
- **Children starting school**
- **Money worries**
- **Relationship problems**
- **Illness**
- **Abuse**
- **Diet**
- **Child leaving home**
- **Bullying**

This list, whilst short, covers the majority of the more common reasons for stress which we hear about on a daily basis, although there are many, many more ... too many to list.

Some people may experience a number of these issues throughout their life, some may never experience any; but what is certain, it seems, is that the more driven and dynamic you are and the more success you experience in life, the more of these you will experience. Some are the things of everyday life that simply cannot be avoided, some are born of indecision and some are issues which require you to walk away from certain situations; all are open to interpretation and are issues which are coped with in a wide variety of ways.

ALL of these issues can be controlled to minimise their affect on your wellbeing, IF you know what to do.

The problem with attempting to use hindsight to identify the catalyst for your anxiety is that you may apportion blame to blameless experiences. This is a dangerous practice.

Many people have given blame to people or situations and have later discovered that they were not to blame at all. It is also common for stress sufferers to apportion blame to what they identify as the catalyst, only to discover that the catalyst had been much earlier and they had wrongly identified something else; often something which had also been caused by the catalyst. For example, a friend of mine always thought that her stress and anxiety had started as a result of her divorce, but actually, her stress and anxiety had caused the breakdown of her relationship. The stress and anxiety had actually started much earlier after the death of her father. It is so easy to be wrong, so it is much easier to move forwards instead of trying to place blame. Hindsight is a great thing, but if the catalyst for your anxiety has been and gone, dwelling on it is a fruitless exercise.

It is vital that you only need apportion blame to CURRENT situations IF you are certain that these are the reason for your current high stress and/or anxiety. The 'here and now' is most important ... the things which you can manipulate, change, affect or improve at this moment in time, the ones that can truly help you to recover for the future.

The most impactful events are those which happen out of the blue or those which you have never been party to before and it is to these which most people react inappropriately. Inappropriate responses are physical, emotional and cognitive (behavioural). It is all too easy to allow these responses to impact negatively on our lives and to let the turmoil you experience take over your logic and spiral seriously out of control.

Create a life map

An important exercise we recommend our clients do is the creation of a life map.

A life map can be easily created using a sheet of blank paper and a pencil with a rubber. All you have to do is start at the top, in the middle of the paper and from that point create a flow chart of all the things that you can remember which have impacted on your life. It is vital that you think of both positive and negative experiences. Try to date them if possible and place them in chronological order, starting at your birth and ending at the present day.

Add things like dietary changes, smoking, illnesses that you can remember, birth of children and so on. By doing this simple exercise, you will be able to build a clearer view of everything you have experienced during your life and from this, many people are able to identify patterns of behaviour or catalysts for stress. Stress often follows definite patterns in some people's lives. Many recently retired people find that stress has started as a result of a change in routine and a lack of activity. Some young people identify partying too hard, drinking or smoking too much or taking drugs as the catalysts.

Also, try to identify any conflicts you may have experienced or may still be experiencing. These could be at work, at home, with parents or siblings. It could be that your self esteem is being lowered by another person, or that you are feeling stifled by your relationship, job, or even children. It could be that you have general anxiety about life and your place in it.

The warning bells

As a reaction to stress you may develop anxiety, panic attacks, insomnia or phobias. You might develop migraine headaches, a bad temper or mood swings; every person reacts differently, but only you know your body, how to read the signs and what seems unfamiliar.

The initial stages of stress usually manifest themselves as changes in mood, behaviour or emotions. Ask your partner or close family members whether they have noticed any changes too; they are usually a good gauge of changes in you which you may not have noticed yourself.

Anxiety, irritability and moodiness are all emotional responses to stress and result from reaching a point where you feel less or unable to cope effectively. Be mindful of how you are reacting to otherwise fairly moderate stressors. Some people also react to stress with dietary changes. Some eat more, some eat less, some binge, some starve themselves. A depleted diet will only serve to add to your body's stress levels.

So if you feel yourself snapping at others inappropriately, or if you are not eating correctly, take a long hard look at what the sources of these changes might be, consider them carefully and make a plan to reverse them sensibly, whilst dealing directly with the stress itself.

Many people attempt to compensate for their sadness with alcohol or smoking. You don't need me to tell you that this is neither a solution or sensible. Both substances are stimulants which will only make you feel worse and neither carries any therapeutic value whatsoever ... if you feel mildly better afterwards, it's short lived and damaging to your long term recovery.

Here is a list of some of the more common emotional responses to stress. Whilst long, there may be some experiences which are not listed.

Anxiety	**Boredom**
Panic	**Lethargy**
Phobias	**Tiredness**
Obsessions	**Insomnia**
Moodiness	**Sudden crying**
Aggression	**Fear of death**
Sadness	**Agoraphobia (fear of being alone or away from a place or person which offers security)**
Indecisiveness	
Social phobia	**Tension**

It is vital that you address any stress issues immediately and therefore that you are able to identify stress as the cause of these emotions and symptoms.

Don't sit back and think that, given time, things will get better; that is rarely the case. Profound improvements can be experienced through some very simple changes in life practice and perception.

THIS IS ABSOLUTELY VITAL:
Stress breeds fear. Fear is anxiety and anxiety lives off your concerns, your worries and your stress. IF you start to believe that there is something else physically or mentally wrong with you, you will start to build belief systems which are called 'catastrophic thinking' or 'what if' thoughts. These are the 'food' of anxiety and once you start down this road of 'obsessive thinking' it is difficult (but not impossible) to pull logic and reason back into line.

Stress can cause a wide variety of strange and sometimes quite frightening bodily sensations and thought patterns, but these are not the signs of illness; they are simply the physical manifestations of stress and/or anxiety in the body ... they are the sensations of fear. Sometimes these symptoms come on rapidly and sometimes they can be there constantly over a number of hours or even days, however, they are transient.

Some symptoms may feel uncomfortable; chest pains, muscle pains, dizziness and shaking for example; again, these are all normal bodily reactions to stress so please don't fear them.

Also be aware that surfing the internet for answers, is not productive, in fact, quite the opposite. The internet and the accessibility to information it gives us can be as damaging as it can helpful. Self diagnosis is not a viable, reliable or sensible option; always seek professional diagnosis, this is vital to your recovery. A doctor will be able to put your mind at rest without subjecting you to millions of alternatives as to what it 'might be', which is exactly what the internet does ... it fuels your fears. A doctor's diagnosis is medical, qualified and informed ... accept it and then move on with the solution, instead of trying to assign blame or to hit on an explanation which requires popping a pill (the easy option) rather than the little bit of hard work it may take to implement the TRUE solution. There is no 'magic pill'.

So, how does stress affect you physically?

The level of stress experienced by each individual sufferer varies dramatically. Some people react with mild aches and pains, others develop high blood pressure, headaches, palpitations or panic attacks; regardless of how stress manifests itself, the condition can be undermined and eliminated using the same techniques.

Here is a list of more common physical stress and anxiety symptoms.

- **Chest pains**
- **Palpitations, rapid heart rate**
- **Abnormal or fast breathing**
- **Panic attacks**
- **Stomach problems (bloating, diarrhoea, constipation, butterflies)**
- **Muscle aches and pain – back and shoulder pain**
- **Insomnia**

- Muscle tremors or twitches
- Tingling in hands, feet or limbs
- Strange sensations or tingling in the face, scalp or neck
- Lethargy, weakness or shaking
- Dry mouth
- Electric shock feelings in body
- Eyes feeling like they are staring
- Headaches
- Urgency to urinate or defecate
- Sweating
- Feeling inappropriately hot or too cold

This list is by no means complete but it highlights the range of symptoms more commonly experienced. If you have stress, or if you have been diagnosed with anxiety disorder, you will find many of these symptoms very familiar indeed.

If you are under a lot of stress but do not have many, if any, of these symptoms, don't worry that you might develop them. Chances are, you won't.

When sufferers become aware of the cause of their condition, it commonly stops developing and starts to retreat. Stress and anxiety need to creep up on you. If your knowledge overrides their build up, it tends to halt their development. The fear of the fear and the sensations themselves are what fuel the stress and anxiety, if you take that fear away the conditions retreat.

The *Stress Free in 30 Days* programme will provide you with many practical ways of minimising the affects of stress; please use them, do not undervalue them. It is all too easy for people who have a grim view of stress and anxiety as some kind of weakness and to 'poo poo' some of the techniques which might just return you to normal. Yoga, Pilates, Tai Chi, Aromatherapy and other treatments, not only relax you, but also build your self esteem and confidence. They have enormous value IF they are relevant and beneficial to you. Let's face it, if someone told you to jump up and down on one leg holding a carrot between your teeth whilst humming the 1812 Overture and your stress would be gone, you'd probably do it.

Stress and anxiety elimination isn't rocket science and our programmes are born of many years of careful development, research and experience with tens of thousands of sufferers. If we ask you to do something, it's because it has been shown to be therapeutic to others ... the things which have no, or little, value, we never mention.

Behaviour which supports stress can cause psychological symptoms

Stress causes behavioural changes in the brain. All the time you change your behaviour, your brain is busily creating new neural pathways of learning which become concreted into your subconscious. These stay there until they become superseded by replacement behaviours and newer neural pathways.

Many people become highly dependent on family, partners or friends, many withdraw socially and some develop phobias or belief systems about their condition.

Stress and anxiety can cause a variety of psychological symptoms; here is a list of the more common ones:

- **Anxiety and anxious reinforcements through catastrophic thought processes ... 'what if' thoughts**
- **Social withdrawal**
- **Agoraphobia – fear of open spaces, fear of being alone or far from a person or place of perceived safety**
- **Anger, aggression, frustration**
- **Feelings of depression. Morbid thoughts. Fear of dying**
- **Feeling like you are losing your mind**
- **Depersonalisation and derealisation – feeling dreamy or as if your mind has left your body**
- **Weird or disturbed thoughts, sometimes of an aggressive or sexual nature, even against your own values or beliefs**

All of these inappropriate thoughts are caused and perpetuated by the behaviour modifications which have occurred as your response to the increase in stress levels. All of these symptoms are normal reactions to changes in body chemicals and are experienced, to a greater or lesser degree, by almost every stress and anxiety sufferer.

It is vital that you understand that none of these symptoms are a sign that you are losing your mind or are mentally ill in some way. It is also vital to understand that all of these symptoms slip away as you start to tackle your stress and anxiety.

Behaviour and our reactions to stress can cause many strange and quite frightening symptoms as discussed previously. We are all built differently and react in a wide variety of ways to similar situations.

By behaving like a stressed person, we become stressed … our behaviour and our reaction to stress catalysts are what programme us to be stressed and for the stress to escalate. By breaking the cycle using behaviour modification, whilst simultaneously changing our perception of the situation and using practical tools to alleviate the stress, a full recovery is possible.

By following the guidelines in our programme, by giving structure to your life and work practices, by nurturing your body and providing it with what it requires in order to function efficiently. By shifting your perception of the stress, you can and will, regain control of your life, eliminate stress and become more effective in every way.

Instructions for the rest of this Book

Proceed through the rest of this book day-by-day implementing the principals described in each chapter fully before moving on to the next.

If a chapter has no real relevance to you, move on to the next. If you are a non smoker for example, the chapter on smoking will have no relevance to you. If you are an occasional smoker, read it. Beware however; be mindful that some chapters may appear, at first sight, to have no relevance to you directly; think hard about whether these have indirect relevance or whether you are misinterpreting a situation. Often third party stressors can have as much impact as direct ones. Maybe a partner or colleague is experiencing a situation which is indirectly affecting your stress levels or mental health; it is as productive to assist this person to remedy this problem as part of your own recovery.

All of the principals are designed to help you to modify behaviours which fuel or perpetuate your stress; by complying to them as closely as possible, you will be eliminating the conscious behaviours which fuel the subconscious 'stress reaction'. Remember, behaviour fuels emotion and emotion regulates how we feel physically and mentally.

Do not underestimate the power of these principals; balance, both physical and mental, is the foundation on which good health is built ... create balance and the mind will follow.

In addition to links to the resources and material mentioned in each chapter of this programme, the accompanying CD also contains other bonus material which you may find useful. To access the CD, please insert it into your CD-ROM or DVD drive on your computer.

If a chapter does not mention a resource, please check the CD to see what is recommended.

DAY 1

Diet

How important is your diet to your physical and mental health?

Put it this way, it's the most important factor in your life that you have TOTAL control over in order to maintain physical and mental well-being; BUT, it is also the most badly executed, poorly managed, widely misunderstood and massively ignored factor too.

If I told you to put diesel in your petrol car, would you? You see, diet is that important! By filling your petrol car with diesel you create a massive rejection process that causes the car to splutter and die ... your body is that engine, your food is that fuel and I can't begin to tell you how VITAL this is!

So many people reject the whole concept of 'correct diet' as ridiculous, mostly based on comments like *"I can eat what I want and never gain weight"* or *"I've got the constitution of an ox"*. These comments might be true to an extent, however, the hidden dangers of food and more importantly, the hidden affects of food, even when there are no apparent immediate reactions, can have far reaching health consequences.

To reject the concept of good diet is to reject the building blocks of wellbeing itself.

In order to gain and maintain physical and emotional balance in which you feel stronger, more alert and able to cope with both the physical and mental exertions of life, it is vital that you maintain a healthy diet. Good diet is a cornerstone of good health and must never be underestimated.

By a healthy diet, I don't mean that you should buy a diet book and stick to it, I mean that you should evaluate what a person of your size requires in sustenance in order to carry out your daily activities, without allowing your body to either receive too much, or too little, food. Too much or too little of the wrong foods, or receiving those foods at the wrong times, can dramatically affect how you feel.

By preventing the seesawing of blood sugar levels, by maintaining healthy levels of vitamins and minerals and by providing your body with the right fuel in correct quantities at the right times, you can feel much better physically and emotionally very quickly indeed.

A balanced diet is vital for maintaining general good health. Avoiding over spicy foods, too many carbohydrates, sugary foods and bad fats are the predictable advice of dieticians world over, but in the quest for eliminating stress, anxiety and worry, it is vital to maintain equilibrium throughout the digestive process and throughout the day and night.

Minimise sugar highs caused by foods such as sugary drinks and carbohydrates by eating smaller, more regular meals of steamed vegetables, fish, poultry and fruit. Avoid piles of potatoes, bread, biscuits and cakes; they produce fast, short lived sugar highs which can leave you feeling tired and shaky as your blood sugar level drops. The buzz word in any diet is 'balance'.

So what should you eat?

There are four main issues concerning diet that I feel are relevant to stress sufferers.

1 **Stress can be made worse by a change of diet**
2 **Diet can affect our levels of anxiety and stress**
3 **Stress and anxiety can affect the way the body accepts foods**
4 **Sedatives or other medications can make changes in the body causing food intolerances and other digestive problems**

I have identified a distinct correlation between change of diet and the onset and perpetuation of stress and anxiety.

Scientists have begun to understand a little more about the role of diet in psychological conditions. They have recognised that anorexia may not be totally to do with self image, but that an element of the disease is caused by a change in levels of certain brain chemicals including histamine released after eating. These can cause unpleasant symptoms, anxiety and psychological disturbances which can cause the sufferer to experience dramatic mood changes, disturbing thoughts, obsessions and other psychological anomalies.

Histamine is a chemical usually associated with allergic reactions; it's inappropriate release into the blood stream can cause unpleasant symptoms including anxiety, palpitations and other unusual bodily sensations and symptoms.

Scientists have become aware that foods can cause a variety of conditions and research is being done to isolate which can be controlled by diet with much emphasis on psychological disorders, which seem to be the worst hit by food intolerances and allergies.

It is thought that even severe disorders like schizophrenia and clinical that depression can be treated or controlled by diet; scientists are currently treating psychiatric disorders with strictly controlled diets and are having remarkable success.

Similarly, stress conditions can be affected by diet … diet may play a vital role in their development and could dramatically embellish the symptoms experienced if not monitored correctly.

Scientists in London have found a strong correlation between mental illness and diet, especially a shortage of Omega 3 fatty acids, which affects the levels of Serotonin in the brain causing depression. The rate of depression in New Zealand, for example, is much higher than that in Japan because the Japanese have a diet rich in oily fish containing fatty acids and in New Zealand, the average diet is based on red meats, much like most of the Western World.

When I first suffered from anxiety I had changed two aspects of my life, I had given up smoking and was on a strict diet to lose a little weight. I believe that these factors contributed to the formation of the initial anxiety I experienced.

There is little doubt that blood sugar levels play a distinct role in anxiety.

As my anxiety increased, I noticed that certain foods eaten at certain times could drastically affect the way I felt. I soon found that by controlling what I ate I could lessen my symptoms.

This is not a psychosomatic symptom of anxiety; it is quite real and effects many stress and anxiety sufferers to varying degrees. This effect is caused mainly by disruption of the system that controls insulin production in the pancreas and is called hypoglycemia. Insulin is the chemical that is excreted by the pancreas in order to control a healthy blood sugar level.

Many people believe that eating sugary food will keep them active and stop them from feeling tired, blissfully unaware that, in fact, the opposite is true. As blood sugar levels peak after eating they drop down as the body uses up the energy created. If you eat very sweet food, the sugar is used very quickly causing the blood sugar level to shoot up and then plummet very quickly, creating the symptoms of hypoglycemia. Coupled with maladjusted production of Insulin during stress and anxiety this combination can leave you feeling very unwell indeed.

When we eat, food is converted into sugar. Insulin released by the pancreas, should keep blood sugar levels constant. When we are stressed or anxious or in withdrawal from drugs including alcohol, cigarettes, sleeping pills, antidepressants and tranquilizers, which can disturb blood sugar levels, the pancreas can produce too little or excessive insulin causing the blood sugar level to fall or rise to unacceptable levels. This can cause many unpleasant symptoms which can be misdiagnosed as stress conditions such as anxiety or even depression.

Most sufferers immediately recognise a definite relationship between what they eat and how they feel and then start a game of 'diet modification' which is often misguided and erratic!

You might find that certain foods affect the way you feel; if this is the case, it is advisable to consult your doctor who may refer you to an immunologist for allergy testing or a dietician who will be able to advise you on a more suitable diet.

During times when your body is under stress it is common to experience food sensitivities. This is due to alterations in the function of the immune system and can also be worsened by the use of certain drugs prescribed for stress and anxiety including sedatives and antidepressants.

It is important that you ask for advice about your diet from your GP or a dietician, but here are a few guidelines for maintaining healthy blood sugar, vitamin, mineral and fibre levels.

A balanced diet should contain carbohydrates, fats, proteins, minerals, vitamins, water and fibre in correct proportions. All of these nutrients are important to maintaining a healthy body. All of the food you eat can affect the way you look, feel and act.

Food provides you with:

- Energy to move and live a full and active life.
- The raw materials your body needs to produce new cells and repair old ones.
- The raw materials needed by your body to make substances used to control important bodily functions. These substances include insulin and adrenaline.

No one needs to be made more anxious by eating foods or adapting eating habits that do exactly that. Here are a few tips for eating foods that will help you to maintain good health and build a sound foundation for your recovery.

- Complex carbohydrates act as tranquilizers by increasing the amount of Seratonin, the neurotransmitter that calms your nervous system. Eating a diet which includes lots of fruits and whole-wheat foods is helpful in increasing your complex carbohydrate intake.
- Tryptophan, a precursor to Seratonin, has a calming effect on the body. Eat a diet which includes turkey and milk, both of which contain high levels of Tryptophan.
- Caffeine can make you jittery and anxious. Replace your daily tea and coffee with herbal teas, especially chamomile which is a very mild sedative.
- Chronic dehydration, however slight, can cause anxious feelings. Drink plenty of water. You can flavor it with lemon or lime juice.
- Frequent, small meals can help to keep blood sugar levels even.

Cut down on or avoid refined carbohydrates.

White bread, sweets, chocolate, cakes and biscuits, fizzy or sweet drinks, sugar.

Eat more un-refined carbohydrates.

Wheat, barley, oats, rye, rice, wholegrain cereals.

Eat more vegetables and fruit.

Loaded with vitamins and minerals and a great source of fibre.

Eat more proteins.

Fish, poultry, meat, egg, milk, cheese, yoghurt, nuts, seeds, pulses and beans.

Bear in mind that some people can become allergic or sensitive to some of these food types during anxiety and withdrawal, if you feel that this might be the case, consult a doctor or dietician who will assist in finding alternative sources of the vitamins and minerals found in the allergy producing foods.

Fats and Oils.

Try to avoid eating fatty foods, they will make you gain weight and are not digested efficiently. Eat more fatty fish like mackerel, these are rich in Omega 3 fatty acids, but avoid fatty meats. Try and avoid using fats for cooking, use olive oil if you wish to shallow fry something.

Vitamins

Vitamins are a very necessary part of our diet although only small amounts are required each day. Vitamins are organic substances that act as catalysts in the metabolic processes of the body. Doctors started to recognise that people deficient in certain vitamins became more susceptible to specific illnesses. For example it was known over 200 years ago that lack of Vitamin C caused scurvy.

There are thirteen vitamins known to us, the top five most important vitamins are vitamins A,B,C,D and E. During anxiety and stress deficiencies in vitamins can become apparent, be aware though that is important to take no more than the recommended daily allowance of any vitamin. Multi-vitamins are available in tablet form from health food shops and chemists. Do not take too much extra Vitamin C, my experience has shown through taking Vitamin C myself and feedback from clients, that it can cause you to feel much more anxious.

Here is a list of vitamins and where they are found naturally in food.

Vitamin A (Retinol): It is contained in foods like eggs, butter, whole milk, vegetables and liver. Vitamin A deficiency can cause night blindness and dry skin.

Vitamin B1 (Thiamine): Foods like fruits, nuts, vegetables, fish, cereals, whole grain and bran contain this vitamin. Alcohol abuse leads to deficiency in Vitamin B1.

Vitamin B2 (Riboflavin): Foods such as liver, milk, eggs and vegetables are rich in Vitamin B2.

Vitamin B3 (Niacin or nicotinic acid): This vitamin is found in foods like cereals, whole grains, vegetables, fish and meat.

<u>Vitamin B6 (Pyridoxine)</u>: A diet of meat, vegetables and bran will maintain the levels of this vitamin.

<u>Vitamin B12 (Cyanocobalamine)</u>: Strict vegetarians may need to supplement their diet with this vitamin as it is contained mostly in fish, meat and milk.

<u>Vitamin C (Ascorbic acid)</u>: Citrus fruits and fresh vegetables supply the body with Vitamin C.

<u>Vitamin D (Calciferol)</u>: Fish, egg yolks and the rays of the sun are the sources of this vitamin.

<u>Vitamin E</u>: Whole grains, cereals, fruits and vegetables contain this vitamin

<u>Vitamin K</u>: Found in vegetables..

<u>Folic acid</u>: A diet that includes liver, nuts, vegetables and whole wheat should provide an adequate supply of this substance.

<u>Pantothenic acid:</u> Liver, eggs, potatoes and vegetables supply the body with pantothenic acid.

Minerals

As with vitamins, the body only requires small quantities of minerals. Unlike other dietary substances both vitamins and minerals do not need to be digested; they are absorbed straight into the blood stream through the stomach lining. Iron is a mineral, which is very important in the carriage of oxygen around the bloodstream, it is the mineral used in the production of hemoglobin and is also responsible for the red colour of blood. If Iron levels are depleted so are the level of hemoglobin in the blood, this causes a lack of oxygen around the body which in turn causes fatigue. Taking a good Multi-mineral tablet to supplement your diet is always a good idea.

Water

Water is vital to good health. It serves to carry substances like oxygen, hormones, vitamins and minerals around the body in the bloodstream. Water also acts as a lubricant in joints, aids control of body temperature and helps cleanse the body of waste products and poisons. We lose a lot of water when we go to the toilet or sweat, which must be replaced by drinking. Dehydration can cause severe anxiety symptoms and impact on our general good health.

Fibre

Fibre plays a very important role in efficient digestion. Fibre is found in fruit, vegetables and whole-meal bread. Fibre is not digested in the intestine and passes through intact serving to cleanse the digestive tract. If you suffer from constipation or diarrhea fibre, may help to improve your digestion.

So, to summarise:

- Eat small meals more regularly. Snack on berries, nuts and bananas which release energy slowly.
- Remember that white bread, biscuits and cake are

quick release foods – they have so little value to a healthy diet.

- Avoid eating late at night instead eat a small snack before bed time to sustain you through the night.
- Avoid sugary drinks, sauces and spicy food and cut down on tea, coffee or other caffeine drinks.
- Avoid alcohol completely if possible, if not, cut down to a quarter of what you would normally consume.
- Drink plenty of fluids (around 2 litres per day)

If you now implement the guidelines I have just outlined, you will feel much better very quickly, both physically and mentally and be preparing your body for a faster recovery from your stress and anxiety symptoms.

Note: Always carry health snacks so that you can top up your energy levels throughout the day. Remember, the more stressed you are, the more energy you are burning so don't forget to re-fuel!

BIG TIP

Eat three large bananas a day, one about 30 minutes after each meal. You will be surprised how much more energy you will have and if you experience any digestive issues such as IBS, stomach cramps, diarrhoea or constipation, bananas can help to soothe and settle the digestive tract.

DAY 2

Alcohol

Let me talk a little about alcohol and how it can profoundly affect your stress and anxiety levels.

You may drink socially, more regularly or not at all; just use common sense to apply this principal to your life ... it will pay dividends.

What is alcohol and why does it make us feel 'THAT' way?

The five stages of intoxication

Alcohol acts like an anaesthetic – the more we drink the more of our brain is anaesthetised! The most common explanation of how the intoxication process works is that the physiological abilities that we learned last like 'social etiquette' are the first to be affected and those that we learned first, for example breathing, are the last to go. In essence, alcohol does these things to us because it's poisoning us … drink enough of it and the ultimate affect of the poison is experienced.

Stage 1 – A social lubricant

After a couple of drinks we are merry. Our bodies react by increasing the heart rate which produces a mental 'high'. The affect of blood / alcohol levels causes the small capillaries in the skin to expand which makes us blush and feel warmer but also lowers the blood pressure.

Stage 2 – The spin

After a few more drinks, we then start to feel light headed and our physical function and reaction is heavily impaired and our ability to reason is affected. These affects are caused by the action of the alcohol on our nervous system.

Stage 3 – "Oy luv you oy do!"

This stage is reached after a few more drinks. Reaction times reduce, speech is slurred and vision severely impaired. The liver becomes seriously overloaded and struggles to rid the blood of the dangerous levels of alcohol you have consumed. With the correct care, your liver should repair itself, but it's struggling to do so effectively after so many repetitions of this damage.

Stage 4 – Taxi?

Now you can hardly walk, you bump into everyone and everything in your path. No one understands you … or wants to!

Your body is rejecting the poisonous alcohol and you constantly need to urinate as it subconsciously decides to release the poison in self-preservation. Your body is dehydrating, exacerbating the affect of the alcohol; this is what causes the inevitable 'hangover' and headaches.

Your stomach and intestines struggle to handle the dehydration too, you get stomach cramps, diarrhoea and sickness as it also tries to reject the poison.

Stage 5 – 'On the edge of existence'

This requires no explanation. The body struggles to stay conscious and is one step away from failing completely! No man's land!

So, what is alcohol?

Alcohol is a lethal poison that can kill in just a few hours … sure it can make you feel good temporarily, but, long term, the affects can be shocking and no one knows what their level of tolerance is … the level of intoxication it might take a grown man 6 glasses of wine to achieve, could be achieved by another with a chocolate liqueur. Add to this very unappealing picture the fact that many people are alcohol sensitive and even allergic and the whole thing starts to look very unsavoury indeed.

Whether you drink every day or in larger quantities over short periods, alcohol can cause anxiety and stress levels to fluctuate dramatically. Many people find that wine is the worst culprit and that during times of high anxiety and stress, it causes much more pronounced symptoms, but every alcoholic drink can cause similar effects.

Alcohol contains high levels of sugar, which has obvious negative affects, but also, the psychological affect of the experience of being drunk or tipsy can alter the sufferer's perception of the world in a way that can cause higher levels of sadness, worry and other emotions. Alcohol consumption should always be minimised for maintaining general good health but in anxiety conditions and times of stress, it is advisable to abstain completely.

If you drink alcohol regularly, you are far outweighing the health benefits that drinking small quantities might bring. The rate of serious illness is massively higher amongst regular drinkers but the health benefits of drinking two or three units of alcohol each week are very widely documented.

So what is a healthy balance? Well, as I have said, two

to three small glasses of wine per week. What about beer and sprits? Well, my advice is to avoid them completely. Beer is full of sugar and spirits are usually mixed with a sugary drink. They have little or no beneficial affect on your health. Alcohol has such a profound affect on us because it is adversely affecting us not because it is creating positive changes.

ALCOHOL is NOT helping you to 'drown your sorrows'... it can't. Alcohol actually has depressant qualities which not only make your mood even worse but ultimately make you wake up the next day feeling worse too.

Minimise your alcohol intake and drink more water-based drinks without extra sugar instead. You will notice the benefits very quickly indeed.

If you stop drinking for one month from today, you will feel fitter, healthier, less tired and more able to cope with everything life throws at you ... try it, you won't be disappointed, that I assure you!

Remember: Alcohol is the number one cause of unhappiness in our society.

DAY 3

Anxiety ... what is it?

Before I tell you about anxiety and the symptoms and thoughts it can cause, let me first of all tell you that some doctors will diagnose anxiety symptoms as stress. This isn't laziness or that the doctors are misinformed, it is simply that stress and anxiety seem to go mostly 'hand in hand', although many people with anxiety have come to me with a diagnosis of stress from their doctor. The whole field is just a bit fuzzy.

Stress is the resultant condition from the pressures of life. To say it's an illness would be wrong, it's not; it's simply a group of symptoms which come together to render the sufferer unable to cope as efficiently as they had previously. The symptoms of stress are wide ranging and can lead to other more serious health issues but generally, if addressed early enough, all stress symptoms can be eliminated without reoccurance.

What is anxiety then? Well, it's any experience of sensations and thoughts, which are present when we perceive fear, but for many people it's more than that. We have all experienced it at one time or another and when it is appropriate, it forms part of one of our most important defences. When anxiety is required it can produce miraculous physical and mental strength but when inappropriate it can cause phobias, panic disorder, multiple symptoms, post traumatic stress disorder and/or obsessive-compulsive disorder.

The symptoms associated with anxiety disorder can range from mild shyness to extreme panic disorder. Symptoms can be varied; from dizziness or breathlessness to muscle tremors, digestive problems and headaches ... the list is almost endless.

So how does an anxiety disorder form? First of all, let me tell you this, anxiety disorders are not mental or physical illnesses, they are behavioural conditions, which means that they have developed as a result of a modification of YOUR thoughts and/or actions ... they cannot form in any other way!

As the initial catalyst for your anxiety produced your initial anxious reaction, deep inside your brain changes were taking place, a learning process, which etches behavioural changes into your subconscious mind. In other words, the more anxious you became, the more your body and mind took on that new level of anxiety as the 'normal' level for you.

It may be that this affects you mostly when you have to make speeches or go on stage but it may also be that you have noticed that your general anxiety level is intrusive, making you feel anxious when you shouldn't. Regardless of what level of inappropriate anxiety you experience, if the anxiety isn't appropriate to the situation you are in, you have an anxiety disorder.

Obsessions are a symptom of anxiety disorder as are panic attacks and phobias ... if you remove the underlying inappropriate anxiety, panic attacks, phobias and obsessions cannot exist. FACT!

So, what can you do to eliminate anxiety, panic attacks, phobias and obsessions? The Linden Centre have treated tens of thousands of anxiety sufferers from probably every country in the world; in fact, I would be willing to bet that we have treated more people than any other anxiety elimination organisation.

What we have discovered is that anxiety disorders can be eliminated using a group of simple but effective techniques in a structured programme that takes no time or effort to implement ... recovery just happens.

We call this programme *The Linden Method* and it is the solution to any inappropriate anxiety, panic attacks, phobias, agoraphobia and OCD. Even depression sufferers benefit hugely, reporting in many cases total elimination of their anxious and depressive symptoms. To learn more about, or to join our programme visit www.stopworry.com and choose your local website from the list of countries. We currently have centres in the USA, UK, Germany, Spain and Denmark.

If you think that your anxiety will just go away, you may be correct, in some cases it does, but there are quite a number of influential factors which need to be simultaneously addressed in order to make a full and permanent recovery, without which, the chances of full recovery are minimised.

Structure, knowledge and support are the three key words when addressing anxiety issues and our experience has shown that by combining these three elements correctly a full recovery is inevitable.

I have prepared a two part anxiety disorder course which you can watch online at **www.stress-and-worry.com/anxiety/** which will explain more about the condition and provide you with links to further information and details of where you can join *The Linden Method* for anxiety, panic attacks and phobias.

The Linden Method
for Anxiety, Panic Attacks, Phobias & OCD

Order 'The Linden Method for Anxiety, Panic Attacks, Phobias & OCD' and receive a 15% discount with this voucher. Quote voucher v1197r

Normal price £117/$177, YOUR PRICE £99/$155

To order on-line, go to: www.stopworry.com

Order by phone: UK 0844 3098 299

To order by mail: Send a postal order or cheque made payable to **Lifewise Publishing** to:

USA – The Linden Center, 381 Casa Linda Plaza #424, Dallas Texas 75218

UK – The Linden Centre, Campion House, Green Street, Kidderminster, Worcestershire DY10 1JF

You can also choose a local telephone access number or your local Linden Method website or office from the lists available at: **www.stopworry.com**

DAY 4

Smoking!
Do you or don't you?

You may not smoke ... if you don't, this chapter isn't for you ... but, if you do, it IS for you and it's important!

Smoking can cause blood sugar fluctuations but also bodily changes caused by its stimulant properties. Smoking cessation is also not advisable during times of high anxiety; adding nicotine withdrawal to the anxiety you are experiencing could be very counter-productive indeed. If you smoke regularly, minimise the daily amount. If you smoke occasionally, stop completely, if you feel you can do so with ease.

There have been many programmes written for smoking cessation but the one which most people find effective is Allen Carr's programme which you can find on our website at www.karmamind.com in the book section.

Smoking does affect your anxiety levels and therefore your stress levels too. By eliminating the negative affects of nicotine you will be adding to the balance you need in order to provide a solid foundation on which to eliminate stress completely.

Habits are the negative manifestation of instinctual behaviour, which you carry out without much or any conscious thought; smoking is no exception. By eliminating negative habits from your life, you gain greater control over your subconscious. It's almost like cleaning out your attic, the emptier it is, the less it weighs down on your house.

Because smoking affects the way you breathe, it can negatively affect the rate and depth of breath, which is pre-set in every person. Stress and anxiety can be brought on by breathing and controlled effectively using breathing exercises; it stands to reason that smoking can affect anxiety for this reason.

So, what's the plan? If you currently smoke over 10 cigarettes a day, try to stay with the 10 a day in order to create balance at a constant level of consumption. Once you have done this, it is vital that you then allow your body to become completely balanced at this quantity. You will not be withdrawing at this quantity but simply maintaining a constant which allows your body to adjust without fluctuation. Your body will be acclimatised to the nicotine it currently receives, so it may be a little uncomfortable or seem a little strained for a few days, but ultimately, it will pay dividends. If you smoke less that 10 cigarettes a day, estimate how many and stick at that quantity. The key here again is balance! Remember that any fluctuations in body chemicals including nicotine or alcohol, (in fact anything we ingest), can cause profound sensations and withdrawal.

You can address your smoking habit later when you feel stronger but for the time being, create balance and control in order to allow your body to recover.

Replace negative habits with positive ones, become passionate about something that will enrich your life, challenge you and ultimately create a feeling of fulfilment.

Just Remember: The next time you find yourself craving a nicotine fix, check your watch and allow yourself only five minutes to dwell on those negative thoughts. Once those five minutes are up you would have finished smoking the cigarette that you were craving. The process is over so forget about it and move on!

DAY 5

Breathing

Do you breathe correctly?

I bet you don't. Most people just breathe ... it doesn't need to be a conscious thing, it just happens ... right? To an extent that is right, the autonomic nervous system takes over breathing for us and generally, it serves its purpose. Sometimes, however, breathing can become disrupted by stress, anxiety, exercise, posture or digestive issues and it is then that we notice the adverse affects that breathing has on the way that we feel.

Breathing can even affect the way that we think. The brain can become disorientated and confused by minute changes in oxygen supply which can lead to drowsiness, confusion and other non specific symptoms – harmless but embarrassing and frustrating for some people.

So I ask you again, do you think you breathe correctly?

There are a number of very good resources and products which can help you to breathe efficiently but a simple breathing exercise can be very beneficial indeed.

What I call the 3:2 technique is a very simple exercise and should form the foundation of your normal breathing technique. Of course if you carry a little extra weight or you are unfit, this may take some practice to perfect but it should become easier as time goes by.

I would recommend doing this exercise twice a day before eating. Sit comfortably in a straight backed chair, if possible wear loose fitting clothes and make sure you are warm and won't be disturbed.

The perfect ratio of in to out breathing is 3:2 so count three on the in breath and two on the out breath over a 60 second period. Before you start make sure that you understand how a breath should feel. Place one hand in the centre of your chest and one on your stomach. Now breathe in. You should feel expansion in both your stomach and your chest equally. This means that your lungs are inflating effectively and optimising the efficiency of oxygen intake.

You should be practising this twice a day to start with for around 10 minutes each session until it feels natural and then increase by 5 minutes every week until you can breathe in this way for an hour or more. Once you have reached this stage, you can do the exercise whilst working or watching TV until it becomes instinctual. At this point you will be feeling very comfortable with this routine. Now you can start to implement this breathing routine as your 'normal' breathing pattern.

Whilst doing this exercise, you could listen to relaxing music and close your eyes if you wish, the meditative element of doing this can be very relaxing indeed and the time will pass quicker. Try to make time to do this exercise and you can even do it whilst at work. Just a minute or two of correct breathing can energise you and relax you in times of stress.

The beauty of this 3:2 exercise is that it can be done as easily in bed as in a bus queue.

The benefits of mastering this breathing technique can be massive. By being in control of your breath, you feed your brain, promote internal calmness, control the fight or flight or anxiety response and prevent stress related conditions from developing – the physical and mental health benefits are enormous.

I would also highly recommend learning Tai Chi or Yoga, both of which use breathing techniques, meditation and controlled movement to promote stress reduction and anxiety elimination. Both can be practised just once or twice a week and the benefits are great. As always, a number of hand selected DVDs are available at www.karmamind.com should you not wish to visit a local workshop.

DAY 6

Exercise

You probably already know that exercise is an important element of maintaining good health, but what you might consider strenuous could be a 'walk in the park' for die-hard exercisers.

If you are experiencing high levels of anxiety or stress, it is advisable to do exercise which doesn't raise the heart rate more than 20-30 beats per minute above your resting heart rate. Doing exercise doesn't mean that you have to send your heart racing like a steam train; exercise should just raise your heart rate to a comfortable level; you don't need to overdo it to experience the benefits.

In many cases, anxiety levels and stress can be adversely affected by strenuous exercise. Walking, cycling and swimming are the best forms of exercise during high anxiety but you must monitor how they make you feel which is dependent on your individual fitness level.

Treating tens of thousands of people with stress and anxiety over the last decade has revealed to us the sort of exercise regimes which are most beneficial to sufferers in order to reverse the affects of stress, strengthen the body, improve cardiovascular function, but also to be enjoyable and relaxing too.

There are two types of exercise programmes that fall into this group, which I have found particularly useful; Tai Chi and Yoga. Both are incredibly effective at providing everything that every person of every age would want from an exercise programme. Both are simple to do, don't require you to leave home, can be done alone or with a friend, can be intensified if required, and include breathing techniques and meditation/visualisation. In addition, once you have become moderately good at them, you can use them for just 5 or 10 minutes each day with dramatic benefits.

Many of my clients now do regular Tai Chi and Yoga exercises. The beauty of these exercises is that you can step out of bed and do two or three before breakfast to prepare you for the day ahead AND they can be done at work, at home, or even on the bus!

The advantages of Tai Chi and Yoga are many-fold. I recommend two DVDs, which many of my clients use as an introduction. Many clients continue to use the DVDs at this level; some decide to take their knowledge further, to join a class or to have private tuition.

Before signing up for a class, it's always better to try something first, so here is the URL to my website where you can read more about, or purchase, the DVDs I recommend.

www.karmamind.com

Linden Method DVD number 1 'Conquer Anxiety and Panic Attacks' includes a complete Tai Chi programme and meditation. It is also available from the above website.

DAY 7

Panic Attacks

You may or may not have experienced panic attacks. If you have, today's session is for you. If not, thank your lucky stars and look forward to tomorrow's session or, you may find this valuable for someone you know who does suffer.

If you have recently, say within the last three months, experienced a panic attack, chances are that you have not yet tackled the subconscious anxious reaction that causes them. Do you ever feel anxious? Do you feel inappropriately anxious, to the point of experiencing physical symptoms?

Panic attacks are the most extreme physical manifestation of anxiety or stress. They can build slowly or hit hard and unexpectedly. Usually, panic attacks cause a number of common symptoms including, chest pain, shortness of breath, sweating, shaking, faintness, racing heart, pins and needles in the extremities, feeling dreamy or unreal, extreme anxiety, weird thoughts and other extreme and frightening symptoms.

Are panic attacks harmful?

No they are not, they just feel very frightening. Panic attacks occur when adrenalin is released by the adrenal glands as a reaction to the perception of extreme danger … when danger truly exists, adrenalin and the anxious reaction are valuable parts of our natural defence system which prepares us to 'fight or flight', when this reaction happens when NO danger is present, it is called an anxiety disorder.

So people might have one panic attack and never experience one again, others develop panic disorder as the result of becoming frightened of suffering another attack. Some sufferers then go on to experience constant high anxiety, phobias and obsessions.

Regardless of the level of anxiety, the regularity of your panic attacks or the thoughts and symptoms you experience, I can tell you right now that you can and will eliminate them completely regardless of what you may have been told before.

Drugs and psychotherapy are not the solution, they can provide temporary respite from your problem, but the only way to permanently eliminate high anxiety and panic attacks is to reverse the process that created them in the first place.

I have helped tens of thousands of sufferers to do this, quickly and permanently using my programme *The Linden Method*. Our team of qualified anxiety, panic attacks, OCD and phobias specialists are available at any time to assist you on the fastest possible route to your recovery. If you wish to join *The Linden Method*, please contact The Linden Centre on one of the telephone numbers on our website at www.stopworry.com or call 0844 3098 299 in the UK. Membership of *The Linden Method* is confidential.

You can also listen to my 'Panic Attack Eliminator' by visiting the following webpage:

http://www.stresss-and-worry.com/panic-eliminator/

DAY 8

Sleep and Insomnia

You know, you probably don't need as much sleep as you think in order to function efficiently during the day. However, for those who suffer with insomnia; there are many things you can do to promote healthy sleep patterns.

Some people wake in the morning feeling refreshed, some feel heavy, lethargic and tired and this can become worse throughout the day. This could be because you are not sleeping long enough or it could be that you are experiencing disturbed sleep.

Here are a group of simple techniques to help you to regain or maintain healthy sleep patterns.

1. Drink a mug of warm chamomile tea 30 minutes before bedtime. You could replace this with warm milk or Horlicks if chamomile isn't your 'cup of tea'.
2. Make sure you are comfortable in bed – bad sleeping posture is responsible for many cases of insomnia. If you ache when you get up or suffer from neck or back pain, it could be that sleeping posture is an issue or maybe its time to invest in a new mattress!
3. Make the bedroom a place of rest only. Put a sign on the door saying 'sleep room' to emphasise this.
4. Be sure to have a light snack 30 minutes before bed time, going through the night without eating is a struggle for healthy people, when you are anxious this becomes a bigger issue.
5. If you lie in bed for more than 30 minutes trying to sleep, get up, make a drink of warm milk or chamomile, make yourself comfortable and snug on the sofa, turn on the TV quietly and watch until you fall asleep … no action movies though … something semi-boring that won't hold your attention for too long.
6. Try relaxation or visualisation CDs to enter a deep state of relaxation, these work wonders.

Poor sleep can create many ailments, none particularly harmful but all quite unpleasant. If you are uncomfortable in bed, if your room is too cold or too warm, too noisy and even if your bedroom is messy, cramped or just simply not a pleasurable place to be, your sleep patterns can be severely affected.

What you wear in bed can also affect your sleep patterns, try looser fitting garments or nothing at all and see how this improves or worsens your sleep patterns.

There are a number of sleep aids available on the market. However, I don't believe anyone should ever need to turn to medicinal intervention for insomnia. My clients have always found that insomnia drugs leave you feeling more tired the next day so it is always best to exhaust all other options first. Below is my TOP TIP ... I only recommend what has worked for me and my clients and having tried most solutions, this is the one that worked best for me and many clients.

Recommendation:

An amazing guy called Matthew Ashenden, who used to serve in the British Military, invented an amazing tool called PZIZZ after researching a way to cure his own insomnia. I recommend this tool to each and every one of my clients. Why? Because it is the most amazing anti-insomnia tool my clients and I have ever used. To find out more about why I (and my family) use PZIZZ every day, both during the day and at night.

This Pzizz gizmo really works – you should really give it a try.

You can also visit these links to download my free visualization exercise audio track:

http://www.stress-and-worry.com/visualisation/

I am certain that these will really help you to relax and get off to sleep.

DAY 9

Environment and Behaviour

Did you know that your environment and your behaviour and your reaction to them, is one of the most important factors in the formation and perpetuation of high anxiety, stress and worry. It is the 'software' that feeds your 'hard drive' (your brain) with the information it requires to 're-set' at a higher benchmark level in your mind.

You know what things in your life are positive influences and which are negative influences. The solution to gaining equilibrium is to implement a filtration process ... we only live once, we need to maximise the positive potential of everything around us to feel fulfilled. Removing negative behaviours and influences is key to our happiness and well-being and to re-programming the subconscious mind.

From the moment we are born, we begin a steep learning curve of behaviour and knowledge outside of our 'in-built' and pre-existing instincts. Everything we perceive through our senses is registered and stored in our brains and waits there to be accessed again as required. All the time this is happening, our brains are building new neural pathways of learning which create and store our experience of life, behaviour and achievements.

If our environment is perceived as negative, our brains develop a life experience pathway around those experiences. Some people get caught up in their negative environment and become part of it. Others rebel against it, developing their own, positive environments and experiences. It's like children who grow up in abusive, alcoholic, smoky environments – they, more often than not, grow up to be just the same.

You know the old saying 'we are what we eat'... well that is true to an extent, however what is more relevant is that 'we are what we think'. Some of the world's greatest scientists believe that we are all part of a whole, at one with the world and that every molecule of our bodies are shared with everything else in existence. By 'thinking' positively, we can affect our own psychology and physiology and these thoughts will influence everything and everybody around us.

The power of positive thinking WILL affect your environment, the people around you and the quality and enjoyment of all your life experiences.

You have the power to take control of how you interact with the world. I have a friend who never stops being jolly, people love to have him around them because his enjoyment and pleasure of life is infectious and he never comes across as sickly or over the top in his pleasure. This person's life isn't perfect, but he makes every moment of every day count. He has few regrets, very few actual problems and has a very fulfilled and happy outlook, which rubs off on everyone he meets. We can all take a leaf from his book.

If you haven't done so already, I highly recommend you read M. Scott Peck's book called *The Road Less Travelled* and the other books in that series.

For *The Road Less Travelled* and *Further Along The Road Less Travelled* by M Scott Peck, visit the bookshop on my website at www.karmamind.com or visit an online or high street bookstore.

The force of attraction is also a very recognised concept, in fact, it has been around for hundreds of years. Recently, a book called *The Secret* which is accompanied by a film of the same name has become very popular.

The Secret is actually a series of devices which can influence the positive outcome of our lives by helping us to focus on those things which can positively affect our lives with very little effort. By following the advice in The Secret, you can become more fulfilled, more successful, more sociable; in fact, you can become who you want to be.

Oprah Winfrey is apparently great advocate of The Secret and uses the techniques to guide her through her amazingly successful career. Many stars and industrialists also use The Secret in their daily lives – the power of attraction is powerful and measurable, it has certainly helped me in my life.

I highly recommend it.

There is a well written step by step programme by Philip Sigglekow which walks you through The Secret and it costs very little.

You can find this by going to my website at

http://www.stress-and-worry.com/thesecret/

DAY 10

Money and Stress

As you probably know, the trappings of modern life can seem very attractive . . . a nice car, a big house, nice holidays and so on. Most people fall into the trap of being predictable, becoming victims to retail madness and living life for the things they can buy, rather than the ones you can't! We have all been there, spending too much money on things that will give us 10 minutes of enjoyment which are then cast aside to make room for the next big idea!

Possessing nice things is addictive; it's a kind of drug, the more you get the more you want. But there's an upper limit usually set by financial constraints and sometimes by lack of vision. Very few people run out of things to buy when money is no object. But why do they need these things? Why are they so important to them? Most people would say that it's because they have something missing in their lives, maybe it is, but I say, most of the time, it's simply the force of habit fuelled by the 'buying buzz' it gives us!

We make conscious decisions in life to either live to work or to work to live and the trappings of either can be suffocating because once you get on that bandwagon, it's hard to get off. But it doesn't have to cause you stress and worry.

It is difficult to balance work and happiness, there is no doubt, however, it is also possible to have enough control over your finances to focus on other more important aspects of your life.

The best way to tackle this problem is 'head on'. Make a list of all your outgoings BUT at the top of the page put your total monthly income after tax. Write the necessities in red ink and the luxuries in blue and at the end of the list add all your outgoings together to create a total. Take this total from your income and that should tell you how much you have left after all your expenditure. If this figure is equal to your income or if you are spending money on credit cards, this could have the potential to add to your stress and worry. If that isn't the case, you may simply need to tidy up your personal cash accounting, making sure that you fall within this range every month and even allowing you to save a little, just in case.

Having full control of your finances is incredibly important, financial concerns account for more headaches
than most other stressors and most of us live beyond or
at least, to our means! This is a recipe for disaster.

You may not be the best money manager in the world,
you may be a spendthrift, you may not earn enough
money for your lifestyle, but you must get a handle on
this before you add to your worry.

At work, I use an accountancy programme to keep
control of all my business income and expenditure, at
home I use a great product that is basically a 'cut down'
version of the same product. I suggest that you buy
some software and start taking control of your finances
immediately … it's just one headache less to think
about every month.

Take control of this. I KNOW it's boring, I know it's
tedious and I know it may take 30 minutes a month to
do … but if your finances are causing you concern, you
MUST do this before it converts from 'worry' to 'night-
mare'!

DAY 11

Relationships

Relationships can be rewarding, amazing and fulfilling. However, on the other hand, they can be destructive, dangerous and frightening! I am not just referring to romantic encounters but family ones too.

Under any circumstance, you need to decide exactly what your relationships bring to you, how fulfilling your relationships are and how they could be improved.

You are in control of who you surround yourself with and it is up to you and you alone, to decide how you can minimise the negative relationships, maximise the positive ones and mend the broken ones. If a relationship is good, it still needs to be nurtured, every relationship including friendships, go through bad times but it is up to you to make sure that the bad times don't last.

Here is my list of 29 points to bear in mind. I am sure that you and I could sit down and write a list of thousands of relationship tips but these are the ones that have worked for me.

1. Try to pay more attention to what your partner says and do so more often. STOP talking and listen more.
2. Be prepared to do something that makes the other person happy … regularly! Go that extra mile to make them KNOW that you care.
3. If you aren't honest and open about your feelings, you are living a lie! Omission is lying too! Speak openly about issues that could affect your relationship, suppressing those thoughts and emotions can create a time bomb.
4. Laugh, smile, giggle and have more fun.
5. Try to pull people into your enjoyment. If you find something that makes you happy, share it!
6. Be able to live your lives independently of shared responsibilities. Find common ground in joining activities not in the chores of life.
7. Stand by your partner through thick and thin … understand that relationships aren't all about fun and games; they are about trouble shooting when the hard times come along.
8. Find out what it is that makes you happy or sad and try to focus on the happy things … this will have a

knock-on affect to your partner.

9. The art of interacting successfully with others relies on your ability to listen to them ... be interested in what others find interesting and if you are not, pretend to be occasionally!

10. Be impulsive. Buy flowers, a surprise gift, a meal out ... it works wonders! BUT, vary the surprise ... lack of creativity means lack of care!

11. Decide on an activity that neither of you have done before and try it with enthusiasm.

12. Sometimes in life we have to do things that we don't like ... sometimes it's for people we love and just because they want us to do them ... that's fine!

13. Ask what they want from you ... if you don't, you may never find out!

14. Try to project your consciousness onto someone else for a while. Try to imagine what it must be like to live your partner or friends life. See things from their perspective, it may inspire you.

15. STOP BEING NEGATIVE!

16. Carry through with every promise. If you don't, you will become known as untrustworthy and disloyal.

17. Being late means that either you couldn't be bothered to prepare well enough to be on time for your loved one or, you just didn't care.

18. Make sure that financial issues don't inhibit your relationship.

19. Be helpful and supportive – offer your assistance as often as you can.

20. NEVER get personal when you have a disagreement – NEVER criticise anyone's family.

21. Make it clear how important your loved ones are to you.

22. Don't ever lie ... you'll get caught and when you do, it looks really, really bad!

23. Anger has its roots in sadness. Look carefully at what angers you and find out if it is YOU or the other person who is to blame or if you are just reacting to your own sadness.

24. Be considerate. Think through the consequences of what you do BEFORE you do it ... it's hard to reverse once you have carried it through.

25. If you disagree, please be sure that you are right ... if there is any doubt at all, end the debate and find out the truth before re-entering into a discussion.

26. Relationships are about investments not bankruptcy. If you take too much out, you'll collapse the bank! Pay in constantly even in small amounts and the relationship will thrive.

27. Relationships are processes NOT events ... they continue and mutate more than any other entity on earth ... they are a learning curve and an experience in one.

28. A relationship is about balance in every way. If the balance is off, the relationship will be difficult to weather. When status quo is reached, the relationship will thrive.

29. THERE IS NOTHING WRONG WITH MARRIAGE GUIDANCE COUNSELLING!

I hope this list will help you to see that there are many things you can start to do today to make big differences to the people you love.

It is all too easy to become lax, bored or complacent about your relationships ... sometimes I hear my friends say *"I just can't be bothered any more"*... what a bad attitude. If they honestly can't be bothered, they seriously need some help!

Take a look at the book *'How to Win Friends and Influence People'* by Dale Carnegie; I strongly recommend it to anyone who wants to improve every kind of relationship – it helped me enormously. You can buy it at: www.karmamind.com

DAY 12

Avoiding Confrontation

Confrontation is probably the largest cause of elevated anxiety. Confrontation can take on many forms; confronting a boss, a relative, a partner, confronting a sudden truth, discovering a secret or hearing shocking news, witnessing a traumatic event ... the list is endless.

Confrontation usually causes anger and sadness and it is common knowledge that sadness causes anger in many cases.

As anger and sadness rise, so too does the level of adrenalin in your blood stream, which causes a flood of anxious emotion, thoughts and symptoms.

Avoiding confrontation is simple. Here are my tips for coping with and avoiding it:

1. Remove yourself geographically from the person or situation that causes it!
2. Count to ten silently and regulate your breathing … slow, rhythmic equal breaths.
3. Go to a place where you can calm down without interruptions.
4. Prevent exposure to the person or situation that caused the confrontation.
5. Decide how best to cope with or deal with the confrontation whilst away from the situation … return to the situation ONLY when you have decided on the best course of action.
6. Decide whether you will benefit from the person or situation long term or whether you are just treading water.
7. If you require assistance, seek out a mediator, a psychologist, counsellor or legal professional in order to help you to rationalise your decisions.

Remember, the only person who benefits from your anger is your opponent, every time you become emotional in these situations you are reinforcing your anxiety and perpetuating how you feel.

YOU hold all the cards. YOU can choose to stay or to go, to react or not to … it is difficult but if you can turn your cheek, you will win out every time.

Situations that drain you are no good for you long term, be decisive about what you are prepared to tolerate even if it means making sacrifices.

Please consider this carefully, it is surprising how many of us suffer under confrontation and don't realise it. It can dramatically increase your stress and anxiety levels, but removing it from your life can create an intense feeling of relief and well-being.

DAY 13

Avoiding Power Sappers

You might ask – who or what are power sappers?

Power Sappers are people who draw energy from you but give nothing in return. These people bring to you nothing but negativity; they suck your energy, your vitality, your drive and your ambition. Power Sappers can be anyone in your immediate vicinity and they usually prey on the easy target. Power Sappers can be your partner, your child, your parent, a friend or a work colleague.

Power Sappers are indiscriminate because they use

anyone to empower themselves. Like vampires they suck other people's life force from them in order to boost their own. Sometimes they do this by undermining you; sometimes they do it by bettering you and then drawing your attention to it; sometimes they just make your life miserable by projecting their emotional baggage and problems onto you.

You know who these people are, but if you don't, ask yourself this about the people you know:

Do they ever volunteer anything to you for no personal gain?

Do they make you feel sad, uncomfortable or fed up?

Do they ever bring anything positive to your life in any way?

Could you rely on them in a crisis?

The answers to these 4 simple questions can be difficult to answer, especially when they address issues with people with whom you should feel close, however, they can be very revealing.

It is vital, not only for your mental health but also for your future goals and ambitions, that you minimise contact with Power Sappers.

Avoid them at all times, they do not positively contribute to your life and serve no purpose. IF they are people that you can't avoid, such as your boss or a work colleague, simply shut down your emotions when in their presence and do not allow them to influence your anxiety or mood … they sap your power to build their own and have no respect for you and your well-being.

Surround yourself with 'power givers', you know who they are; they are the ones that feel good about themselves and make you feel good about yourself. They are the people who empower you, inspire you and make you feel positive about all you do or want to do with your life.

If you need to be structured in your decisions about who these people are, make a list and try to identify exactly what each of these people bring to you.

So, what do you do once you have identified these 'rogue friends'? You minimise contact with them, you devise methods to undermine their negativity, you bring them into environments where they cannot openly undermine you without ridicule … in other words, you stop their behaviour in its tracks before it gets you down.

I know this sounds simple and in reality, it's much more difficult than it sounds, however, it is vital that you stop the Power Sappers … let them self-destruct instead of destroying you.

I love a good book. The principals in *Families and How To Survive Them* don't only apply to family members; it's an interesting book for most people who struggle with relationships. Go to the bookshop at: www.karmamind.com

Day 14

Balance, Challenges, Enjoyment & Meaning

Balance ... what does that mean?

Balance, or status quo, is when work, leisure and family enjoyment and fulfilment are in the ratio that most fit your circumstances; BUT, more importantly, this ratio must mean that none of the three factors are compromised in any way.

If any do become compromised, this may not affect you

directly, but it may affect those you work with or care about.

Let me give you an example.

Danny is married with three children. He works in the city as a sales agent and works 5 days a week. He leaves home at 6am and usually returns at around 7pm just as the children are going to bed. As his wife gets them tucked up, Danny eats his dried out meal. When all is tidied away and the kids are asleep, Danny reads his emails, plays a little online poker and falls asleep on the sofa. Danny plays golf most weekends … just a few rounds with his colleagues. Once a week Danny pops out for a 'pint or two' and sometimes goes for a curry on the way home. Danny's wife Gilly is a stay at home mum who can't afford to have a hobby as money is allocated to other things. Gilly's day is usually spent cleaning, tidying, preparing clothes, making packed lunches, collecting and dropping off and occasionally Gilly stops for a cuppa with her friends. The family usually take two weeks holiday in the UK, but occasionally take a package trip abroad for a week. Gilly used to play racket ball regularly but is now too tired and unfit after having the children.

OK, do you get the picture? I don't think I need to say any more about this family … the imbalances are so obvious. I call this The Butterfly Effect. The Butterfly Effect is actually a theory of quantum mechanics, which basically says that a butterfly flapping its wings in South America will affect the weather in central Europe say. OK, it's an extreme concept but one with deep scientific basis. Similarly, what we do, even things which we perceive as the trivia or 'norm' of our everyday lives CAN have a dramatic knock on affect ... they can affect others in ways that we don't even perceive and may even be directly detrimental to our lives without us even realising it!

But the question is, what do you do about it? Danny works hard for long hours, but so does Gilly. The kids hardly get to see their dad during the week and at weekends he plays golf. Gilly misses him but Danny can't stand the kids arguing and screaming all the time.

The answer is in balance. Danny can't stay home, he needs to earn money, but when he gets home, instead of heading straight to his computer, he could set 15 minutes aside to read to the children; they have contact with their dad and two people are happier already. When the kids are in bed, Danny eats his dinner and he and Gilly can spend some time discussing their day before they snuggle up on the sofa to watch their favourite show. At weekends, Danny could play golf late afternoon, that way the kids don't feel deserted on a Saturday morning. Instead, the family could visit friends or go on an outing, just to create a family time and a definite break to the working week that the kids can look forwards to.

The watchword here is structure. It's easy to fall into bad habits, which mean that all family members have little to look forwards to. With variety, plenty of family time, regular 'Danny and Gilly time' and two loved kids, things become so much simpler.

Reassess the structure of your week. Be honest about whom or what benefits from your time at all times.

Try to see what you do from other people's perspective; it may be that what you do works for you but not for others ... be aware that when others are not happy, this can come around full circle and bite you on the butt in other ways. A subtle change to these habits can cause dramatic changes, which create greater flow in your life and the lives of those you care about.

Importantly, the old routines will become memories, you will all be happier and so will the people around you.

Here are the questions I ask clients to ask themselves to identify and eliminate the things they do which can be changed for the better.

- Does my work life require modification?
- Can my work life be made more effective?
- If my work life is as ordered as it can be, who does it affect and in what way?
- How can I soften the impact of my work life on those around me?
- Who benefits from the time I am not working?
- How can I maximise the benefits that I can create during the time I am not working for those I love?
- What can I do to make those I care about KNOW how much I love them?
- How can I spend more time with my partner doing the things we used to love to do together?
- Do my hobbies mean that others experience any loss or

'down time' in their routines or enjoyment?
* What do all of these modifications bring to me?

If you truthfully answer all of these questions, you will find that there are changes that you can make which dramatically change your enjoyment of life and undermine any stress you experience.

DAY 15

The past, present and future of YOU

You have experienced the past, you are living the present and the future is the only thing you can influence.

Memory has a purpose; it's a filing system for your experiences, both negative and positive.

Negative memories need to be filed away in the archives of your mind allowing you the opportunity to create positive memories, which can then become your focus.

It is so easy to dwell on the bad things that happen to you and some can be very bad ... life is full of pitfalls and sadness. However, those who navigate it successfully are those people who are able to identify and file those experiences efficiently in the library of their minds and move on.

We can do nothing about the things which happen without direct input from us, they are the concern of others or 'fate' itself ... if you believe in fate.

The things that we can influence are those things that should most concern us and it can be our job to positively or negatively influence those things if we so choose ... the path is ours to take, we just need to be decisive and move forwards.

Live for tomorrow, not yesterday and make today the first day of the rest of your life.

Those who hang onto the past never experience a positive future.

When I moved back to the UK after several years living in Germany, I walked into my local pub to find the same people stood in the same place, talking about the same things as they had previously. However, there was a marked difference ... they only talked about the past, they rarely spoke of their goals or ambitions and they were pretty scathing about mine!

I was shocked at how these people hadn't seemed to have moved on, they even recount stories of what we did previously, sometimes over 10 years before! I can't remember most of what they talk about because so much has happened in between but because their experiences are limited, they harp on about the same old stuff!

This is the first day of the new you ... make it count!

DAY 16

Goal Setting

The basic principal of goal setting is simple.

Take a blank sheet of paper and write down your short, medium and long term goals. Be realistic about your ability but stretch your expectations so that the goals are challenging for you.

Never be disappointed by not achieving your goals, instead, be impressed by your ability to chase them.

Try everything; take every opportunity that arises and regret nothing, its all part of the challenges and your personal enjoyment of life.

1. Be able to make decisions
   Being successful comes from being able to make the decision that success is your ultimate goal and making a plan to lead you there. Waiting for chance, luck or good fortune to shine on you could prove to be a very long wait! Only YOU can plan and execute success.
2. Being focused
   Keep your eye on the ball ... it's a moving target so don't take your eye off it! Your ability to remain focused has a direct affect on your success.
3. Do you know what failure is?
   It's one of the outcomes of having 'tried'... its part of the road to success! However, if you don't utilise the lessons learned by failure, it will be time and resources wasted.
4. List your goals.
   As I said before – make a list of your goals and stick to it. You may think you are 'Mrs or Mr Memory' but you can't remember everything.
5. Make plans.
   Remember the five Ps. Proper Planning Prevents Poor Performance – one of the main rules in successful business and life strategies.
6. Delegate and question.
   No one knows everything so delegate, ask questions, collect knowledge and don't be afraid to ask for help.
7. Get off your butt!
   If you just sit around and wait for the success bus, you'll see it pass by you so quickly and you won't be able to jump on.
8. Be kind to yourself.
   Throw yourself a 'Scooby snack' every time you have

been successful! Even self-awarded rewards are empowering.

9. Don't let the side down – even when the side consists of just you!

    You are your team. Don't allow anyone to influence your goals, ambitions and work ethics. You are in charge, you make the decisions and you reap the ultimate benefits.

DAY 17

'Work Time' and 'You Time'

So what is YOU Time and Work Time? Here's the low-down.

Selfishly claim a section of each day, say one hour, to do things for you. You could have your nails done, have a massage or simply read a book – the choice is yours.

Remove yourself from interruptions, from noise and stress and make that time yours, every day. Ask a friend or partner to assist you with this if need be … it's the only link you have with the old you, pre-children, pre-work, pre-marriage … it's your 'grass roots' time.

Putting it in simple terms, our lives are made up of three elements, these are: Work, Sleep and Leisure. Many people feel that their lives consist of too much work, not enough rest and sleep and very little leisure – does this ring a bell?

There exists a way of assisting you to redress that imbalance by regaining equilibrium in your work life. This is called a 'Personal Timeline' and this is how to construct one. First of all, draw a straight line on a (landscape positioned) piece of paper. Make the line about 6 inches long. This line is our 'day line', representing a 24 hour period, so break it down into 6 equal parts, each section represents a 4 hour period.

Now decide how much sleep, on average, you require each night … if this is 8 hours, mark in an 8 hour period on your timeline, so this equals 2, 4 hour sections.

Now, do the exact same thing for the amount of time you work each day. Then, also, mark your travel time to and from work on the timeline.

Now you can plainly see that the remaining area on your timeline is your 'play-time', the time that you can spend doing whatever you wish. Now, I understand that most people have children, partners and other family members and issues to mark onto the timeline, but for now at least, let's presume that you have 4 hours per day for leisure activities.

This timeline chart will help you . . .

- Ensure that your work doesn't run outside the 'work' area of your timeline . . . if it does, ever, make moves to redress this imbalance. Work should never be allowed to over-run into leisure time.
- Gradually work towards shortening your work time block so that you can enjoy more YOU time.

The lessons that you can learn from this kind of exercise are important, such as:

Learn to combine your activities. Let go of your 'life habits' and rituals – be more spontaneous. Learn to refuse when others make demands on you.

Successful management of your personal timeline will result in you making more time for you and your loved ones and also provide you with a greater sense of 'balance' between work, leisure and rest.

Ask yourselves these questions:

"Is this the best use of my time?"

"Am I going about this task in the right way?"

"If I stopped doing this, what would the outcome be?"

Be honest about the answers and I think you will be quite surprised.

If you want more control over your life and more time for you and your loved ones, this technique can help to make all that a reality. The only additional skills you require for making this work are discipline and patience, but it will pay dividends.

DAY 18

Disaster or Opportunity?

Let me first of all tell you this ... COPING IS NOT AN OPTION!

If you are just coping, it means that there are still unresolved issues to address.

It is vital that after a trauma, no matter how insignificant the trauma may seem to others, we learn how to THRIVE.

The experience of thriving means that the traumatic

experience has absolutely no detrimental affect on the sufferer's life.

OK, memories may exist, they always will, however, it is vital that they are rendered as such and stored appropriately in order to minimise their impact at all times. Like the bereavement process, painful memories should be allowed to weaken with learning techniques that allow the healing process to take place. If the sufferer is constantly fed reminders of the painful experience, it is doubtful whether they will ever be able to move on and thrive.

The most effective techniques for coping with painful traumatic events involves a structured timetable of activities which not only create focus and diversion but also builds on and embellishes your life experiences in order for you to find fulfilment and happiness powered by the painful experience and the new found hope you pull from it.

We all experience negativity in life, it's part of being alive, but what survivors do is to use the negative force to find new life energy.

When I recovered from my anxiety disorder, I previously made the decision that living my life in painful, frustrating limbo just wasn't good enough. I told myself that IF I was going to stay like this forever and then drop dead, I might as well do something in the meantime, no matter how scared I was ... and I was pretty scared believe me.

Through the chest pains, dizziness, horrible thoughts, panic attacks, stomach problems and many other awful complaints, I decided that I would get up, get dressed, go out and challenge myself to take the best photographs that I possibly could and it was this which tipped the scales for me on my road to recovery.

Of course, an anxiety disorder cannot be eliminated simply by taking a few snapshots, but it was a major factor in my recovery, that's for sure.

You have a choice; you can decide to allow your negative experiences to overwhelm you and be the guiding force for the remainder of your life, or, you can decide to create success from disaster and drive yourself forwards … it really is your choice. Will you be a victim or a success? Your choice … 100%

If you reject the challenges of life and give in, you can only rest assured that YOU and only YOU have put yourself there. It's all too easy to play victim, but from the outside, you look weak and from the inside, you feel it! Don't sit around waiting for something to happen or for someone else to pick you up and dust you down because, chances are, it won't happen. NO ONE ELSE LOSES OUT … that I promise you, no matter how sorry you feel for yourself, I guarantee no one else feels as sorry!

Make that choice today … create energy from your experiences and drive forwards. You will become a hero and everyone else around you will look up to you as a winner, a guiding strength and an inspiration.... instead of someone who simply GAVE UP!

Sometimes, out of trauma, loss and sadness, new opportunities are born!

I have, this week, read a book that I enjoyed immensely. It is a wonderful tale of how a rich, overweight New York Lawyer turned his life around after a courtroom heart attack. The transformation was miraculous and the lasting peace and happiness he found was incredible. The book is called *'The Monk Who Sold His Ferrari'*.

If you are interested in reading his amazing story, you can buy it through my online store at: www.karmamind.com

I hope you decide to buy it; it really is an amazing story of triumph over adversity.

DAY 19

Confidence

Regardless of your ability or achievements, have confidence in the decisions you make and take responsibility for the consequences.

Be able to apologise for wrong decisions and be prepared to adapt to changes. Confidence comes from not fearing the outcome of your actions. Only you can take control of this, but if you do, you will be able to do and say things that are usually the reserve of super achievers.

Here are my rules for increasing your confidence.

1. The biggest problem with having confidence is over-coming the 'what if?' question. The 'what if' question is the one that undermines our confidence, by creating a 'fear of consequences'.

   What if I try this building project myself? Well, the house could blow up! That train of thought is common in those who lack confidence because they are focusing on the worst possible scenario. People who have confidence are fully aware that there could be negative consequences, it's just that they only focus on the positive ones! It's about changing your mindset and NOT fearing the outcome. KNOW WHY? Because everything can be put right!

2. If you haven't done something before and you are lacking confidence, you can do two things to give you a confidence boost right away. You can give it a 'trial run' and you can use 'role play'. By practicing what it is you have to do, even driving to the place and running through the activities you have to do, you minimise your anxiety by familiarising yourself with it before you have to do it 'for real'.

   Role-playing with someone you trust really helps too. It doesn't matter what the situation is, simply pretend that you are in it and try to 'live it' as best you possibly can. This really works.

3. I have a saying – in fact, I have two! One is 'don't reinvent the wheel' which is self explanatory and the other is 'stand on the shoulders of giants'.

   Why try to start from scratch when you can replicate what others have done? It doesn't make sense to have to create and test, change and re-test until you get it right, if someone has already done all the testing for you! Very few things are NEW; usually someone has done them before and that being the case, copy them!

There are so many successful role models out there in the world, instead of trying to beat them, use their success to fuel your own!

4. We are what we do (not just what we eat!) In other words, behaviour makes us who we are. If you act timid and weak, you will be timid and weak instinctually. If you act strong and confident, even though you may not feel it at first, you will become confident and strong. From now on you are not YOU, you are Brad Pitt or Angelina Jolie PLAYING THE PART OF Confident YOU! Do you understand? You are now an actor playing the 'confident you' and very soon, that behaviour will become part of you!

5. Make sure that your perspective of the current situation you are faced with is realistic and justified. Try to see it from someone else's point of view, would they cope in the same way or do the same things? If you can look at the situation objectively and be honest with yourself, usually, things are much better than they at first seem.

6. Don't be a 'yes' person. Ask for what you want and need in a respectful and intelligent manner and you will usually get it!

7. That internal dialogue you have with yourself every time you are faced with adversity – IGNORE IT! If you can't ignore it, try to imagine it in Donald Duck's voice or Bugs Bunny's … suddenly not quite so serious is it?

If you implement these rules and use them constantly, you will find that your confidence will grow.

DAY 20

Feeling fulfilled

Feeling fulfilled is the key to happiness, stress, anxiety-free living and to your enjoyment of each and every day.

Feeling fulfilled is the result of a combination of realistic goal setting, removal of stressful influences and personal achievement, in fact every positive influence you can gather on your journey.

Feeling fulfilled is simpler than you think. It requires a little planning but apart from that, as long as you stay convicted to your need for personal success, regardless of how that success manifests itself (business, sport, money etc.) you shouldn't go far wrong.

So what can you identify in your life that could potentially make you feel fulfilled?

Is it career success? Money? Sporting achievements? Your relationships? Children/family? Holidays/travel? Educational achievements? Language abilities?

Write a list of what YOU need to achieve for YOU. NOT a list of the things you need to do for others, although this might also create a feeling of achievement for you … if it does, add it to the list.

Be realistic about what you can achieve but don't underestimate your abilities. So, if your wish is to be a deep-sea diver, that might work out, but if your wish is to visit the Titanic without the aid of a diving bell, it's probably best to rethink. What I am saying is … know your limitations but push them!

Feeling fulfilled could be easier than you think. Take some time alone. Go to a quiet place … the park is always good. Place yourself under a tree, for example and close your eyes. Take a deep breath in and picture yourself happy and contented doing what your imagination tells you. Make a note of what you see. Repeat this exercise to discover the true you – the 'you' that is free to do all the things that you need to do FOR YOU.

It may be that you discover things that you want to do that might upset others or might not 'fit in' with other people's plans. You then have a decision to make … to drop the idea, to go through with it and ignore the consequences, or to compromise in some way. There is usually always a solution if there is conflict.

I can only suggest things to guide you to this ultimate state of fulfilment … there is no 'magic wand' that can award you fulfilment … you have to attain it yourself.

I hope that this might have sparked inspiration in you and that soon you will be under a tree, seeing your successes in your mind's eye and making plans to see them through.

Take a look in the personal development section of my website at: www.karmamind.com

Also, this website has an amazing product – I won't say too much, read for yourself how it could apply to you. This product has been very highly recommended by a number of clients. Go to: http://www.stress-and-worry.com/passion/

DAY 21

Organising yourself

Organisation is key to living life stress free. If you allow your life to become a tangled mess of string, tightly bound up and almost impossible to unravel, you are asking for disasters to happen.

My father always said to me "make a list"... he was right, making list of all that you need to achieve in a day or week or month is probably the most important stress-busting tool I ever used. It teaches you to focus on, prioritise and execute your tasks in an organised and structured programme each day, nothing is more effective. Striking through your completed tasks is very satisfying!

If the problem you confront is made up of multiple elements, break it down into its parts and ask the same questions again. Note down the answers on a sheet of paper for reference later.

1. Identify the problem EXACTLY. Define the problem accurately and objectively without ambiguity. Be mindful of the fact that emotions can give us distorted views and make some problems seem insurmountable.
2. What has caused or created the problem to arise? List what you perceive as the catalyst of the problem; list as much detail as possible.
3. What could the solution be? Brainstorm a list of solutions, but do this quickly, spontaneously, off the 'top of your head'. Now, study the list and prioritise and number each item in order of importance.
4. What course of action can you now follow in order to solve this problem? List every source of help, every resource and every approach you need to solve this problem efficiently and then make a strong decision about how much time you will need to execute this solution.
5. Identify your ultimate goal. What are you hoping to be the outcome? What would be your ideal solution

and how would this end up? Also, ask yourself whether your problem is worth the investment or whether it would be better to abandon this problem. It may be that the problem isn't worth solving.

By truthfully addressing these 5 questions, you will be able to structure a results focused solution to every problem you encounter, no matter what the scale. Instead of 'troubleshooting', you will be able to calmly take on any problem and conquer it with confidence; avoiding the, sometimes inevitable, stress and worry it can cause.

Don't be a slave to problems; problems are challenges and are just an opportunity to use these five questions from now on.

PERFECT PRACTICAL PLANNING (PPP)

This method allows you to itemize and prioritise activities in a structured form, allowing you to methodically work through goals set by you. Routine and planning are the two key words for organised, stress free work and life practices, implementing this structured approach will pay dividends.

It is important not only to plan future work but also to intelligently analyse completed work. This method will allow you to do that effectively.

The PPP form is a practical way to organize your work structure. There follows a simple page structure to work to but it is best to add and modify the form to suit your individual needs. It is important that you limit the list to one page though in order to focus on and to condense your objectives; it can otherwise become too messy and disorganised.

Allow yourself a small amount of time each week to look back at the previous week's form and to add to the next week's form.

The goal of this process is to save your precious work time, to focus thoughts and to put structure into your work practices.

Your ability to plan and structure your work routines improves with time. With these forms you can build a weekly picture of your life, your achievements and your goals and follow the development of your work practices and your achievements. A simple one page form can consolidate your thoughts and provide a structured platform to cope with most tasks competently. Focus and structure are the keys to successful work practices. Try to be structured and exact with the questions on your form, this will provide more targeted answers.

Use your form as the foundation on which to structure your working life. It can become the cornerstone of maintaining focus and poise and ultimately achieving a fulfilling and stress free working life.

Building your PPP Form

1. What have this week's achievements been? What is the most outstanding achievement this week?
2. How have I progressed with: a) leads/sales, b) production, c) cash flow, d) contacts, e) ideas?
3. Have I responded to all enquiries and correspondents? Is everything up to date?
4. Is my work on target to meet objectives/goals/expectations?
5. List new contacts? List any future appointments set up?
6. Did I successfully achieve all that I could this week? What do I need to revisit/mend? What went well?
7. Did I eat well, exercise and try to be healthy in my approach to work?
8. Make a priority list for next week?
9. Make a list of all the people you need support/help from? Have you prepared for and set up all meetings for next week?
10. Is my priorities list being adhered to?
11. Is this weeks goal plan being adhered to and achievable?
12. Where or who are potential pitfalls? List the solutions to these also.
13. What could I do to ensure that next week is as successful? Am I prepared?

Organisational skills are paramount to stress free, structured life practices . . . if you ignore them you risk being subjected to chaos and negative outcomes.

It is your choice, but I believe that if you adhere to these ground rules, your stress will fade away.

Stress is a state of mind ... pressure causes stress if you don't 'own' it. Make the decision today.

DAY 22

Conscious Choices

You have a conscious choice to make when confronted with adversity; you can either decide to allow the problem to propagate, grow and invade your life, or somehow, you can salvage an opportunity from the wreckage.

When you apply this principal to some of life's more serious catastrophes, it can seem a little mercenary. However, the people who move on, deal with and leave tragedy behind and make a success of their lives are those who can take advantage of every pitfall.

Humans experience, on average, between 25,000 and 50,000 unique thoughts per day. If 90% of those thoughts are negative, what affect will that have on your enjoyment of life? EXACTLY, you will end up, depressed, disheartened, unfulfilled and fed up!

Cognitive therapy is commonly used in the treatment of depression and centres on the theory of 'you are what you think'. So, if you are able to take control of your thoughts and then, in turn, your actions, you can quickly become a 'positive thinker' and the knock on affect through your life can be quite profound.

So, how do you do that? Well, here are some guidelines.

- You don't need to change your FEELINGS to affect the way you think … it's easier than that and, in fact, the complete opposite!
- Keep a notepad nearby and write a list of all the negative thoughts you have during one day … this will quickly make you aware of just how negative you are! I think you will be shocked. As you write each one down, think about how you could have perceived the event/thought differently or how you could have shifted your viewpoint to produce a different outcome. Be aware of your 'opinions' as you keep this list … opinions about yourself and others are vital to identifying your negative moods and their affects on your self-esteem and your trust/opinions of other people. You could make two columns in your notepad … column 1 – negative thought, column 2 – alternative thought. This way you can quickly identify and keep tabs on how to amend your thought processes. Soon,

your behaviour will change and the positive thoughts will outnumber the negative ones.

- STOP focusing on problems. Problems are opportunities to apply your ability in order to find a solution. NO problem is too large ... in a month you will have forgotten what the problem is!
- STOP CATASTROPHISING! If you programme yourself to focus on the 'worse case scenario', usually, regardless of the actual size of the problem, its affect on you will be maximised! Listen to the words you use; words such as NEVER, CAN'T, WON'T, ALWAYS etc. NOTHING is black and white ... there is always an area of grey from which to salvage some positives! Of course, if you are one of those people who thrive on being the victim, this advice won't help you – you have condemned yourself to a life of self-inflicted misery. That's not to say that you can't change that fact but if you do, it's going to mean being very honest with yourself and most 'psychological self-masochists' won't do that!
- Ask someone you trust to tell you whenever you are doing or saying something negative ... you could even help each other. If this is someone you spend a lot of time with on a normal day, this could prove an excellent exercise for improving your environment, office relationships, friendships and work productivity! A negative environment will produce negative results generally.
- Try This: Next time someone asks "How Are You?". Answer "Fantastic thanks and what about you?" Positive reinforcement does work – before long you will feel as good as you proclaim!
- Once you have identified when, how and about what

you are being negative, focus on how you can change these things. It could be that definite events or people are the catalyst for this negativity – make decisions about how YOU can change your reaction to these in order to make you feel better. Be selfish about what you want and manipulate others and situations to get what you need from them by being positive and calm. Next time a catalyst appears – mentally knock it down and move on.

- A good reminder of this is a rubber band worn around the wrist. Every time something negative happens, twang it to remind you that you MUST react POSITIVELY!

I have recommended a product many times before and whilst it is not intended to change your negative thought patterns, its affect is quite amazing. It's called Holosync Technology and was developed by the Centerpointe Research Institute. This technology is simply amazing, both my wife and I use it daily and recommend it to everyone who simply wishes to create focus in his or her life.

This product is not hocus-pocus; it's scientific and very powerful indeed.

If you implement the ideas outlined in this chapter, you will immediately start to see how a simple change in your thought patterns can have a very positive impact on your life.

DAY 23

Collect Happiness

Are you aware that many accumulated 'small pleasures' can be more satisfying than one big one!

Trust me, a constant stream of pleasure is a lot more satisfying than one big large explosion of pleasure! This can be applied to so many things!

Like all good things, pleasure usually builds slowly and in fact, most of the pleasure is in the 'build up'.

You can choose to go for the 'big finish' or to continue with the on going pleasure. The excitement of many of life's fulfilling experiences is in the build up, the preparation, the challenge and most of the time the end result is over too quickly.

By planning your life around a constant flow of small pleasures, even just taking ten minutes to have a cup of tea and a biscuit mid afternoon, you can unlock a very positive mental attitude.

If your day is a stream of stress and chores, punctuated at the end with a sense of relief as your head hits the pillow, you are going to spend much of your day focusing on your bed! That's just not positive now is it?

By making a day plan with regular breaks, regular YOU moments, fun things, listening to music, walking in the park, chatting to friends etc. you can make your day much less tiresome, more interesting and more productive.

Remember when you were at school? Presuming you all had a fun school life, regardless of the intensity of the learning element, you always looked forward to going to school so that you could show everyone your new toy, new hairstyle, discuss last nights TV, play and have fun.

Sure, the school day was filled with boring stuff, however, the glimmers and moments of fun in between made the whole thing bearable. It is up to you to find out what makes you tick, identifying things that could offer moments of relief and making sure that you build them into your daily routine.

Try being a big kid … it really works. Our adult lives are constructed from endless responsibility, chores, work and structure. Think back to the last time you actually had real fun … fun that penetrated through the steel hull of your daily chores and infiltrated your life positively.

Chances are, you don't remember the last time you felt that way. You have an opportunity to change all that.

Evaluate your life on paper. Write down all the stuff you HAVE TO DO. Then write down how long those things take. Calculate how much spare time you get in amongst those chores and how much time you have outside of that time. Really study your timetable and discover what your life is really all about.

You have a choice to make – Live or survive?

Choose to live and you will balance your necessary chores with your enjoyment of life! This IS NOT a dress rehearsal, one day it will be too late to change.

THAT'S YOUR RESPONSIBILITY!

DAY 24

Ignore Your Weaknesses and Draw Upon Your Strengths

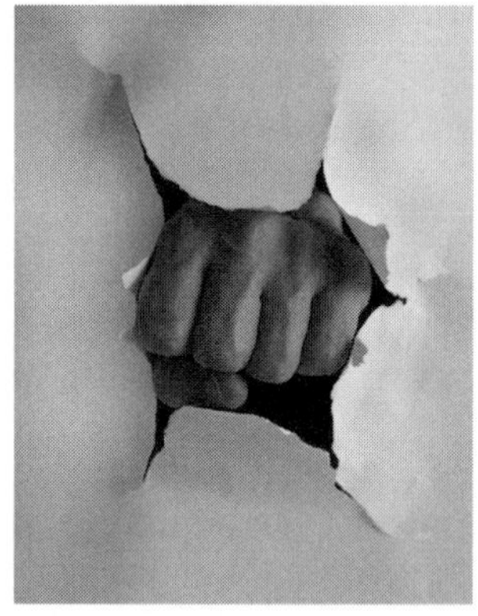

When someone asks you what your strengths are, do you give out a little chuckle, become embarrassed and underestimate your abilities? If you don't, either you are confident in your abilities or you are masking your lack of confidence with a practised script!

I asked this question to 40 applicants for a job recently and most of them giggled, dipped their heads and then lifted their eyes in search of a clever, inspirational answer.

It's not a difficult question but most people struggle with it. Why? Because its something most people don't consider … ever.

We all have weaknesses but those who focus on them tend to use them as a benchmark; a point that should never be exceeded. Confidence is the main issue amongst these people, but lack of knowledge about the person they should know best is equally to blame in many cases in other ways.

Do you know what your weaknesses are? Do you know what? Other than the extreme fears of life and any physical constraints, you shouldn't actually have any! And any you do have should be made into reasons to compensate.

I reached a point after I recovered from my anxiety, when I said to myself... "You've been through the worst, it can't get any harder than that, now it's all downhill and you have to take EVERY opportunity life throws at you".

This was a serious turning point for me. I decided that if I was going to find my ultimate happiness and fulfilment, I had to experience as much as possible, fill my life with new challenges and learn new skills.

I started by accepting every opportunity that came along - "Charles, can you do anything about this broken chair?" Without thinking about it, I'd say "yes", knowing full well that I hadn't got a clue where to start … but I would learn!

I accepted every challenge and it paid off. I found my ultimate happiness and I am living it right now.

My son, Charlie, has a condition called Duane's Syndrome in his left eye. His vision in that eye is very poor and the other eye is very short sighted indeed. So you'd think his ball skills would be bad, his hand to eye coordination would be affected and he would fall and trip regularly … NOPE! He has been spotted by a football talent scout, he is top of his class at gymnastics and I can't remember the last time he fell over … he is 5 years old!

What is the story to be learned from my amazing child? Triumph over adversity, use what you've got to its full potential, focus on your abilities and build on all of these things. I am not going to recommend a book … you are the master of your destiny … you decide what you need to do.

So I ask you once again … what are your weaknesses?

(Subtle clue to the answer: "I have none")

DAY 25

Beauty ... where is it?

When was the last time you felt invigorated and awestruck by something beautiful?

It's probably been a while. Modern humans are so caught up in the trappings of modern life that the simple pleasures fall by the wayside. It doesn't matter where you live or what you surroundings are like, you can find beauty everywhere ... and I mean everywhere.

The eyes are the most sensitive organ for capturing emotion. Sure it's nice to be touched, to smell or eat something good but ultimately, seeing something good arouses immediate thoughts and sensations … some pleasurable and some not so!

We are blindfolded by life. Our routines mean that all we perceive in life isn't all we see. We see beauty everywhere but it is filtered out and overwhelmed by the focus we hold on drudgery.

When I was recovering from my anxiety disorders, I bought a camera! Best move I ever made! It wasn't expensive, just a standard film camera with a zoom lens. It made such a difference to my recovery that now I recommend photography to all my anxious clients.

WHY?

Have you ever looked through a viewfinder? What does it do? It makes us focus on a slice of the world. Then it makes us select the most attractive shot possible to immortalise on film.

Try it. Go out into the garden and find the most beautiful shot possible. The very action of focusing your consciousness through one eye into a confined area (the frame), has the affect of diverting all your conscious thought onto what fills it!

NOW you are seeing beauty. What affect does that have on your mood?

Photography therapy is a recognised therapy now but is not practised very widely. There are many books about the practice but the most practical one that I have found is called *'God Is At Eye Level'* and you can buy it from my website at:

www.karmamind.com

The book has no religious significance, for those who were wondering; it's just a great example of what you can achieve when you really look at the world.

Of course, photography is simply a technique that worked for me and many of my clients. You don't have to follow my lead on this one. You may find it just as easy to go to the park and look around you.

BUT … please don't underestimate the power of this technique. Seeing beauty is the most powerful, practical technique that you can use with no cost, no effort and very little time which leads to permanent lifting of the spirit and improvements in your enjoyment of life. A great stress reliever!

We all do it, we all ignore beauty, miss it or render it insignificant in our lives but it's there waiting for you to interact with … why waste that opportunity.

Stress busting in its purest form … now go hug a tree!

DAY 26

Posture

Most people neglect correct posture and on the whole never experience any negative effects until quite late in life, backache and neck pain being the most common of these.

If a person with high anxiety and stress also suffers with incorrect posture, this can have a profound effect on the intensity of their anxiety symptoms.

I have already discussed that breathing is a very important factor in the treatment of stress and anxiety disorders. If you correct breathing patterns, anxiety levels will fall … it's not the CURE but it is an enormous help!

Posture has a profound effect on breathing, if muscles and bones are compressed, a certain amount of internal restriction has to be expected.

Stress and depression can cause a person to become guarded, they feel subconsciously that they need to protect themselves from danger. Like a scared hedgehog that rolls itself into a ball to protect its soft vulnerable belly, we too tend to sit with our arms crossed, our legs tucked tightly to our bodies and our shoulders and torso rolled at the waist when we are anxious or depressed.

This posture is achieved totally subconsciously but is seriously unhealthy; it compresses internal organs including the heart and lungs and it inhibits good circulation and causes muscle, tendon and nerve tension and often pain.

If you feel that you are doing this, try and correct it. The more you are aware of what you are doing, the more you can practice good posture. If necessary, ask your relatives and friends to tell you when you are doing it, if you change this you will feel better almost immediately.

In our modern lives we are less likely to stand, walk and run for long periods. Over the last one hundred years, human habits have evolved quicker than at any other time in history; we have more stressors, life is faster, more expensive and definitely more competitive. Our bodies, however, have not evolved to accommodate these changes in life practice. This can cause incompatibility between physiological makeup and activities. Over sustained periods of physical and mental pressure caused by these incompatibilities, physical problems can develop which manifest themselves as stress.

Physical activity promotes more effective circulation, muscle fitness, cardiovascular fitness and healthier lungs. Lack of exercise, bad posture and poor air quality in our modern offices can be very damaging. The average person that works in an office probably sits for at least five to six hours of the working day and only moves to walk to the coffee machine, to grab a quick cup of stimulant, just to kick-start that adrenaline.

Sitting in an office chair is not bad, but should only be done for short periods with activity in between.

The sitting position compresses the torso and the organs below the diaphragm are pushed upwards towards the chest cavity, restricting the lungs and heart. If you are overweight, this compounds the problem. Shorter shallower breaths are taken and blood oxygen and blood carbon dioxide levels are compromised. Most of my work is done seated at my computer. I have recently bought a kneeling chair, which has improved my posture, but I used to feel terrible if I had been seated for long periods. The discomfort was not always apparent immediately, but would sometimes carry over to the next day showing that breathing can be altered drastically and persistently over extended periods.

Correct posture – chest expanded, back straight, lungs and internal organs relaxed.

Bad breathing and posture could explain many of the symptoms associated with work related stress. It doesn't take too long for a person's natural breathing patterns to be altered enough to cause some unpleasant symptoms including anxiety, panic disorders or depression.

Couple incorrect posture with radiation from monitor screens, poor quality, recycled air or air conditioning, lack of fresh air, central heating, coffee drinking, long hours and a demanding workload and it is easy to see why the epidemic of 'work stress' related illness is developing.

Posture for correct breathing – to improve bad posture, it is important to find a seat that keeps the back straight, try not to lean onto the desk. In this position the chest cavity is at its optimum size whilst sitting.

Physical activity helps to maintain good circulation and allows the skeleton, muscles and other bodily tissue to stretch, opening up the joints and allowing the body to breathe. Try to avoid drinking too much coffee or tea, as they are both stimulants. Lessen the effect by drinking a glass of water every time you have a coffee or tea. Make sure you get copious amounts of good quality, fresh air, open a window if you can and try to get outside of the building during break times if possible. If you feel that you are suffering from stress at work due to excess workloads, you must talk to your boss or union, if you belong to one. Do not allow yourself to become ill because of your workload; having time off work because of stress should not be an option, you should not be in a position to be subjected to inappropriate stress and workloads; if you are, talk to someone about it.

The Alexander Technique

The Alexander Technique is a method that redresses incorrect breathing, posture and movement and was invented by Frederick Alexander, an Australian actor.

Alexander realised that his ability as an actor was affected by his posture and devised techniques to improve both posture and breathing technique; it also improves balance and coordination. The technique teaches the use of the appropriate amount of effort for a particular activity, giving you more energy for all your activities.

It is not a series of treatments or exercises, but rather a re-education of the mind and body.

The Alexander Technique can help a person discover a new balance in the body by releasing unnecessary tension. It can be applied to sitting, lying down, standing, walking, lifting, and other daily activities.

Excess tension in your body can cause a variety of unpleasant symptoms including backaches, sore neck and shoulders, carpal tunnel syndrome, lethargy, sleeplessness, resistance to stress etc.

People of all ages and lifestyles have used the Technique to improve the quality of their lives. The Alexander Technique has been taught for over a century and thousands of people worldwide have gained newfound health by practicing the exercises.

There are Alexander Technique resources which I recommend highly which can be found on my website at: www.karmamind.com

DAY 27

Massage

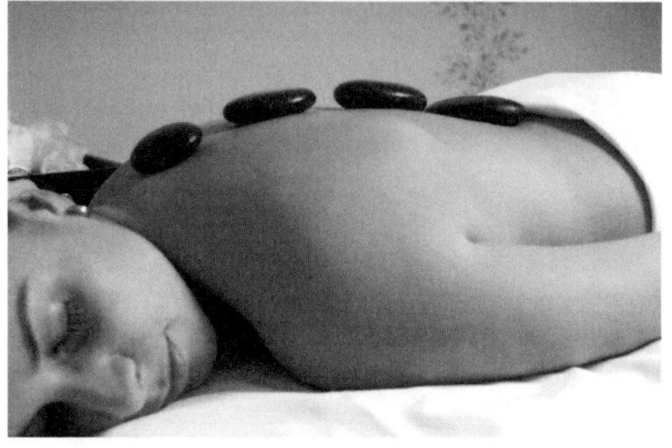

I cannot express how important and beneficial massage can be in the treatment of stress related tension, muscle pains, mental release of tensions and stressors and general wellbeing.

There are several treatments I highly recommend.

I have a regular massage, which lasts about 40 minutes at a local holistic health centre and the benefits are incredible.

Full body and/or aromatherapy massage are incredibly

beneficial. If you suffer with psychological or physical stress, full body massage, with or without aromatic oils is fantastic. It is not only relaxing to the extreme but also softens up all of those tight sinews and muscles. If you can't afford to get a regular massage from a professional, get your partner to do it for you.

Hot stones massage. I really enjoy this therapy, just because it feels great. The benefits are not as great as a full body conventional massage but give it a try if you would like.

The benefits are amazing regardless. A head massage is a quick fix; it really does have an amazingly positive affect on how you feel.

Massage isn't difficult to do at home; you can even do it to yourself. I was at a health and beauty exhibition in London earlier this year, taking a look at lots of new products when my wife stopped at a stand where the visitors seemed to be queuing up to try the products. The stand sold massage machines.

The man on the stand asked me if I would like to try one, which I did. I have tried many massage machines in my time but this one really hit the spot! I didn't hesitate to buy it. I was then also asked to try an eye massager that can be worn backwards to massage the back of the head and neck … I tried it and my eyes, tired from three days at the exhibition, felt refreshed … so I bought one of those too!

The Acumag all over massager and the eye massager

are simply wonderful and can be used alone or with your partner. They are powerful and versatile; you can just apply more pressure if you need a firmer touch.

If you would like to try these two machines and find out why I lock myself away for 20 minutes every day with two vibrating machines … go to my shop at www.karmamind.com and go to the massage section. If you wish to read up on massage techniques, visit the books section where you will find some great guidance books.

DAY 28

Alternative Therapies

I am not going to bore you with information about how waving fig leaves over your body whilst you are bandaged in soured goats milk wraps on a bed of Japanese volcanic mud will purify your chakras.

What I do want to do is give you a practical synopsis of one or two more therapies that I have tried and that I have recommended to my clients, which have helped them and me in some way.

I want to tell you the affect they have and what you can expect to experience … no flannel … just facts.

This list is in order of effectiveness starting with the best.

1. Reflexology. Unless you fly through the roof when you have your feet tickled, reflexology is very relaxing and certainly seems to have a therapeutic affect. It claims to manipulate organs around the body through the soles of your feet. Sounds far fetched I know, but I have experienced a number of occasions when ailment have been detected by the practitioner by massaging my feet. This is a great stress reliever and doesn't tickle at all. You can have the practitioner do light touch reflexology or a more firm approach.

2. Indian Head Massage. I can't say enough about this practice. If you have never had one, try it! Ask the therapist to massage your face and forehead too; it's amazing for migraine, neck pain or that 'stuffy head' feeling and great for clearing sinuses. You can have it done with or without smelly oils.

If you suffer from stress symptoms, tension and anxiety, here is my timetable for minimising their effects:

Once a week, full back, neck and shoulders massage. Pro or by partner … it doesn't matter. With hands or using a massager.

Twice a week minimum, Indian Head Massage by pro or partner.

As a treat – full body aromatherapy massage once or twice a month.

Once every two weeks – reflexology.

If you can't afford all of these treatments, take it in turns with your partner. Resources for all of these can be found on my website if you wish to have a go. Go to www.karmamind.com or find a local shop that stocks good quality oils and massagers.

DAY 29

Hobbies and Fun

Do you have a hobby? Do you have fun?

Why don't kids get stressed? Because they have too much fun!

They laugh, they joke, they take very little seriously and they are, on the whole, blissfully unaware of the complexities and frailty of life.

We as adults, on the other hand, know all too well about the complexities and frailty of life, don't we? Bills, loans, jobs, kids…it's surprising really that we remain sane at all.

I have many friends and they all fall into 2 categories, those who have fun and those who don't! OK, occasionally, Matthew might let his guard down and chuckle out loud, but, most of the time, he sits there quietly sipping his low alcohol beer. Does he have a hobby? NO. Does he go anywhere without his family? No. Does he tinker in a potting shed? No!

You see Matt, like many men and women I know, is a plodder ... he's a survivor but he just dilly dallies through life, solving problems as they arise, never challenging himself, or anyone else for that matter, always towing the line.

Now, you see, I don't tow the line ... I'm the one who manufactured the line and rented it to everyone else, because, I do have fun and when people are with me, they have fun too ... but it wasn't always like that ... in fact, when I was younger, I was the designated driver, the bloke holding the ladies coats as they danced with my friends in the disco ... I was 'the sensible one'. I had fun ... sort of! But nothing like the fun I have now.

I tinker with my old Austin car, I take photos, I go to track days and race around, I go to motor racing days, I walk up BIG hills, I am an activist, I socialise and I HAVE FUN!

Do you?

IF NOT, WHY NOT?

Everyone needs a release ... a place where they can go

to do or not do, anything they wish. A POTTING SHED, metaphorically speaking of course.

Many people already have potting sheds … they call them Yoga classes, pottery, life drawing classes, photography classes, hiking etc.

So, if you haven't got a 'potting shed'… find one! I guarantee to you that by just taking that little bit of time to do what it is that makes you happy, your stress levels will reduce and your sense of well-being and your conversational skills will increase quickly.

If you already have your 'potting shed', just check that you haven't built it on top of anyone else's … selfishness is a relationship exterminator!

I can't find a hobby for you … only you can do that … my hobbies are my lifelines … go for it!

DAY 30

Look and Feel Great!

Look in the mirror. What do you see? How do you feel about you? Do you like what you see? Does what you see make you feel a certain way?

If, like most of the billions of humans who walk the earth, you are self critical, if you are affected by the way you look, if you mention things you would change about yourself in conversations and wince when you look in the mirror, then it's time you took the bull by the horns and did something about it.

I am not suggesting you re-mortgage the house to pay

for cosmetic surgery, that you go on a crash diet or dye your hair pink ... what I am suggesting is to take some time to decide what you could do tomorrow to make you feel better about the you in the reflection.

It could be so simple.

When was the last time you had a hair cut or colour. Are you going grey? Does your hair colour work for you? Is your makeup done correctly? Have you changed it in the last year or two or is it the same now as in 1976? Do your clothes reflect your age and fit you correctly? Does that goatey still make you look dapper?

There are a million questions I could ask you that could identify what you are doing now, that you can change tomorrow, to make you feel MUCH better about yourself immediately!

Most stores have personal shoppers, advisors and stylists. USE THEM. Have your hair done, go and get a free makeover at your local department store ... the cosmetics counters will be glad to ply you with every new product designed for your 'skin type' available. Take advantage ... get some advice.

Men, do the same. Feeling fresh and well groomed will have a remarkable affect on your self esteem ... trust me, just getting a quality hair cut and shave can make you feel so much more positive.

You see, if you don't like what you see in the mirror, you will behave differently ... less confidently, less positively. Body image is how you feel about yourself and you probably see yourself very differently to how you are seen by other people.

Work on things that you can do RIGHT NOW to make you feel better about you and make plans to do the things that may take a little longer.

Conclusion

OK, if you have reached this part of my programme and still feel stressed, its because you are either too lazy, can't be bothered to implement this advice, or there is something you have missed.

I am not saying that you can cure all of your stress overnight, you probably won't; but if you implement the advice contained in this book, you will be taking long and positive steps towards significantly reducing your stress and anxiety short term and developing the positive habits and the changes in your perception of your world, to achieve long term success.

Don't be a slave to your perception of your world. Bring structure to your thoughts, love and happiness to your life and fulfilment to each and every moment you live.

You need money to live, that's a fact, but, you don't have to be a slave to the environment you live in ... you have the ability and the right to modify your environment, to focus on the positives, ignore or expel the negatives and to become a more fulfilled and happier person.

This is your life; as far as we know, we only get one ... make it count, starting RIGHT NOW!